WRITERS WRITING

Edited by
JENNY BROWN
and
SHONA MUNRO

· EDINBURGH ·
BOOK FESTIVAL

MAINSTREAM
PUBLISHING
EDINBURGH AND LONDON

The moral right of the authors has been
asserted

First published in Great Britain in 1993 by
MAINSTREAM PUBLISHING COMPANY
(EDINBURGH) LTD
7 Albany Street
Edinburgh EH1 3UG

ISBN 1 85158 495 1

A catalogue record for this book is available
from the British Library

Typeset in Palatino by Litho Link Ltd,
Welshpool, Powys, Wales

Printed in Great Britain by
The Cromwell Press, Melksham, Wiltshire

CONTENTS

THE WRITING DAY

WRITING EQUIPMENT

WRITING FOR CHILDREN

THE WRITER'S WORLD

BACKGROUND TO WRITING

INSPIRATIONS

Foreword

Gore Vidal once observed that audiences at the Edinburgh Book Festival are more than usually responsive, eager to engage authors in discussion. That it is such a rewarding platform for authors has ensured that the Book Festival continues to be a powerful magnet for those involved in the creative process. While Gore Vidal attributed it to there being so many advocates and lawyers in Edinburgh, we would put it down to the enormous fascination here about all aspects of the writing process. Where do writers get their ideas from? When did they first put pen to paper? Which authors influenced them? How did they first become published? Do they use a word processor or pencil? Since the Edinburgh Book Festival started in 1983, six hundred authors have been quizzed about why they write and the same questions crop up again and again.

This book seeks to give some of the answers. To celebrate ten years of the Book Festival, we invited a number of authors who have appeared with us to reveal more about their approach to writing. The result is an illuminating – and entertaining – examination of the creative life in all its rich diversity. The authors reveal where they work (Elspeth Barker's earliest scribblings were in a hen-house; Maya Angelou writes in a hotel room accompanied by a bottle of sherry and a deck of cards), what they write with (green ink for Joan Lingard, and for Candia McWilliam the sharp precision of an Eagle Verithin), and why they write at all. They discuss family encouragement and suppression (two authors had their early work burned by parents), and the moment of inspiration – exactly like catching a cold, according to Angela Lambert. The trials of the creative process are also reflected in the witty drawings provided by leading illustrators. We give our thanks to all those who have generously contributed to this volume.

Writers Writing will inspire those who write, encourage those who aspire to write and engage anyone for whom all kinds of reading are a positive pleasure.

Jenny Brown (Director 1983–91) and
Shona Munro (Director 1991–),
June 1993

First Attempts

Illustration by Michael Foreman

ELSPETH BARKER

Elspeth Barker was born in Scotland and educated there and at Oxford. She is the widow of the poet George Barker and has lived for the past twenty-five years in north Norfolk. She has five children and two grand-children. As well as continuing with her writing, Elspeth Barker teaches classics at a local girls' school. Her other occupations include rearing children and animals, waiting for AA Relay, and leaning on the Aga rail.

Previous titles include:

O Caledonia

ELSPETH BARKER

Tales from the Henhouse

'Tis pleasant, sure, to see one's name in print;
A book's a book, although there's nothing in 't.

I remember these lines of Byron from childhood; and the thrilling image of the dark leather cover, the gold lettering. Imagination ventured no further; the pages remained blank. Later I read of Colette's father's unpublished book, always kept on a high shelf, an object of awe to his children. Whatever his shortcomings, he had *written a book*, and, one day it would be off into the wide, eager world. In stealth and solitude, after many years, his daughter dared to draw it from the shelf. Nothing in 't. There is a yawning abyss between wanting to have written and actually writing.

As a child I wrote, variously in the derelict henhouse, the loo, or the glory hole under the stairs, perilously illuminated by candle stubs. It was clear to me that this had to be a secret activity, although my mother, who had always read aloud to us, was fervently encouraging. She said, 'You must go for long walks to gain inspiration.' One of the attractions of writing was that it was an indoor occupation; fresh air and exercise had no part to play. Also I didn't want anyone to see what I had written. Mostly I wrote moody verses about pine trees and winter seashores, or vengeful ballads inspired particularly by 'Binnorie':

> The eldest cam' and pushed her in . . .
> Sister O sister, sink or swim . . .'

Prose works concerned horses and dogs. I had almost finished a novella, 'Buccaneer, the Story of an Exmoor Pony' (influenced more than a little by *Black Beauty, Lorna Doone, My Friend Flicka, Bambi* by Felix Salten and a host of others), when my mother found it, stole it and lost it. I loved then the physical act of writing, the imprint of the nib on the fresh paper, the pleasurably painful inky bump on my middle finger. I always wrote with my fountain pen; writing was too sacred for the banalities of dip pen and inkwell. My pigtails used to fall forward and drift across the page, leaving a smudgy wake. I knotted them together and held the ends in my teeth. My shoes had to be laced up very tight before I could begin.

At horrible girls' boarding school, and at university I continued to write, extremely awful verse supposedly in the manner of Hopkins or Yeats. I stalked the streets of Oxford shrouded in lengths of purple taffeta, hoping to resemble Maud Gonne, or Emily Brontë, who is unlikely to have had a use for purple taffeta. After Oxford I went to London to write my great novel. In fact, all my energies were taken up by waitressing in Lyons Corner Houses and dodging about the underground in flight from a lunatic Nigerian who claimed to have married me by proxy. Back in my freezing, lightless garret I began to realise that I knew nothing and had nothing to say. I lost two stone and wrote not a word.

Then came marriage, and babies, lovely babies, cherubim. I couldn't have enough of them. Writing faded into a dim aspiration, a Maybe one day. Suddenly they were all grown up. There was time; I could stay awake after nine o'clock in the evening. I could even read books. But with the passing years had come self-doubt.

> If the sun and the moon should doubt,
> They would both immediately go out,

observed William Blake (or something to that effect).
'There are twenty-four hours in the day and twenty-six

letters in the alphabet. All you have to do is rearrange them,' urged my husband. Robert Louis Stevenson wrote *Dr Jekyll and Mr Hyde* in three days while ill in bed. None of this helped. My oldest daughter, now working on a glossy magazine, telephoned. 'Mum, you know how you're always going on about your hens. We're doing an Easter feature with hen *things*. Write something.'

'I will, I will,' I cried, but did nothing.

She telephoned again. 'I'm coming home this weekend. Have you done your hen piece?'

'Yes,' said I. Driven by panic I wrote three thousand words overnight on the glories of hens I had known. The glossy wanted a hundred rather different words to thread around photographs of egg-cups and hen tea-cosies. I sent my article to *The Observer*, who took it and printed it, and asked me for more. Then came a magic, dream letter from the fiction editor of a publishing house. She had read my pieces; was I thinking of writing a book? If so, she would be very interested. I could not believe this letter's existence; I stood washing clothes at the sink and kept looking back at it on the kitchen table. At one point, in fact, it disappeared and I thought I had indeed been dreaming; it turned up again among my son's car documents.

I sent two thousand words off to the publishers. A week later, on Robert Burns' night, I came home from work to find a letter waiting. In mortal fear I made beds, brought in firewood, fed animals, put supper on, before I opened it, hoping that God would look kindly on my simple toil and reward me for it. He did. My almost non-existent novel had been accepted. Outside a hurricane was blasting about. What cared I? I drove ten miles through blackness and falling trees and lagoons of ice water to buy celebration drink. In the morning there were six trees down around our house and no way out. There was nothing to do but write.

In a year's time, also, oddly, on Robert Burns' night, the book was finished. My exhilaration then was even greater than it had been on the night of acceptance. I had done what I had set out to do. I knew that it would be published. I had written a book. It seemed as marvellous and metaphysical as calling a bird down from the sky. I expected nothing further;

it was enough in itself. Over that year I had discovered one or two things which surprised me, although they may seem obvious. I found that writing came to me in spasms, sometimes for two or three weeks at a time, often for much less. Between those spasms were ghastly periods of the familiar self-doubt and fear. When the book was going well I lost all sense of time and place. Once I wrote for thirteen hours and thought it had been three. I was convinced that I couldn't do dialogue and prevented my characters from speaking for one third of the book. Then I discovered that it wasn't so hard as I had thought. Having only written articles before, I enjoyed the leisurely pace of a longer form, and the sudden realisation that I could make the characters do anything I liked, moving them back and forth through time. Possibly the barren periods are inscrutably productive; I write in longhand, and do no rewriting. Often I don't know what is going to happen next and the pen surprises me. Moments like these make the hours of solitude and cold, the anti-social nature of one's task, exciting and worthwhile. Just as often I stare at the blank white sky and the blank white paper and wonder why I ever thought writing was a good idea. This is a mystery. I can only explain it as an addiction to words, a constant nagging in the bleak recesses of the skull. At the beginning of the day I will do almost anything to avoid the moment of picking up the pen, even when things have gone well the day before. I'd rather wash the kitchen floor. I'd rather unblock the drains. But then, on a good day, to write gives me more happiness than almost anything I now know. And all you need is an A4 pad and a pen.

TOM POW

Tom Pow was born in Edinburgh in 1950. After studying at St Andrews and Aberdeen, he taught in Edinburgh, London and Madrid, and now works in south-west Scotland where he lives with his wife and baby son. He is the author of two award-winning books of poetry. In 1988 he was awarded a major Scottish Arts Council bursary. His play *The Execution of Mary Timney* was commissioned to celebrate the tenth anniversary of Radio Scotland. In 1992, Canongate published his account of travels in South America. In 1992-93 he was the Scottish/Canadian Writing Fellow based in the University of Alberta, Edmonton. He is currently preparing his third collection of poetry, *Red Letter Day*, for publication in 1994.

Previous titles include:

Rough Seas
The Moth Trap
In the Palace of Serpents – an experience of Peru

TOM POW

Letting go the Handrail

Once I mastered my d's and b's, and forgot the nightmares my first teacher Miss T gave me with her ruler-slaps for my confusion, my writing career began. Perhaps my most important, though derivative (teacher told us the story) early work was 'The Rolling Plum', published here for the first time:

Once upon a time there was a lovely juisy plum on the top of a plum-tree and that plum wished to see the world one day a gused of wind came and the plum shaked and shaked and off he came but all the other plums were fritend. but the plum only laught and who wurys about that I'm off to see the world oho off we go said the plum. and off he went and a kitten saw it and becan to chase it but it found a leaf to play with insted. And the plum rolled on and on. He met an old woman and the woman gave chase ohoho off we go. But the woman gave up. Then he went on and on until he came to a medow where some children were having a picnic one girl notist the plum and began to run aftir her but they becan to feel tird and sat down for breth. Then he met a boy fishing and the boy began to chase it he thot that he had cot it but he had not. The plum had fallen down a hole. And he slept and grou into a luvely plum-tree.

For most of my school life, compositions were the work I enjoyed most. I carried their titles home with me, precious as secrets, and was a willing captive to them in my small bedroom, looking out over the summer garden with its three neat lawns and small avenue of apple trees (my mother and father gathering grass cuttings in the green evening light).

This was not the case with irregular Latin verbs or mathematical formulae: though to my regret, particularly regarding a science, I never ventured deeply enough into any other subject to feel confident about letting go the handrail of dogged rote learning. But in composition I felt I could swim; and, after I sensed the career teacher's face strain into a mask when in first year, a butterball of a boy, I told him yes, I could see myself as Peter O'Toole in *Lawrence of Arabia*, I thought I might just be a novelist instead.

The plain fact that I couldn't seem able to finish any of the novels I started with such enthusiasm in a myriad of notebooks (the fourth chapter always seemed to defeat me) did not connect with my unfitness for the form – though anyone reading 'The Rolling Plum', that early manifestation of Magic Realism, might guess that the author would eventually experience difficulty in the area of character development.

Still, I retained my commitment to story-telling and write-a-description-ofs until one hot summer study-break for Highers, I began to write poetry:

> The corrugated earth lies open,
> Its virginal ruts welcome the seed,
> The seasons father the young bread on,
> The ploughman's thrust in, the earth will now bleed.

And, as it poured out of me, I realised with a certain feeling of disappointment (as I saw my audience melt!) that poetry was to be my true medium.

For over twenty years now, I have been writing poems. Apart from the adolescent notebooks, which I threw away in a pruning fit, I have notebooks, folders, drawers and half a filing cabinet full of the material which has come to fruition with the publication of two precious plum-trees.

But why do it? What's the point?

To all such questions, I could give a different answer each day – and have done, much to the consternation of the television interviewer who found her recent research on me invalid on the day. Besides, these are not questions to which I devote a great deal of time. My father is a painter, mostly of musical abstracts, and creativity was always a natural part of (home) life for me. Because of this, I warm to the comments of the French artist Julius Bissier, writing in his old age that 'the desire for validity has become for me one of the most dubious human traits. Anything that is a thing has validity. And all the more so if it has come into being without effort – because then it arises from inner necessity. Here alone is the source of validity.'

It is answering such as 'inner necessity' that has always seemed to me the most important thing about writing, or any other art. Doing it. Again I think of my father who, as a young painter, took part in the first surrealist exhibition to be held in Scotland before the war; who had refused to compromise the excitement he felt, while on a travelling scholarship, about modern European painting, and later about the American abstract expressionists.

'A little recognition would have been nice,' he has said more than once, as we stood before a fresh canvas ('Aye, it's a good one that . . .'), 'but look at Cezanne, van Gogh . . .'

Or Emily Dickinson, who wrote, 'Being a poet is all; being known as a poet, nothing.' The first part of her credo can only make one (me) feel inadequate; the second hypocritical. The truth of the whole is caught more warmly by Yeats:

> Be secret and exult,
> Because of all things known
> That is most difficult.

These thoughts, I suppose, once would have constituted a second-hand faith for me, until I had an experience, which allows me to speak with a more genuine self-knowledge.

When I told Stephanie Wolfe-Murray at Canongate that I was going to South America – the plum that wanted to see Machu

Picchu – she immediately responded, 'Write us a book!'

I had been awarded a Scottish Arts Council Writers Bursary whose purpose was simply to enable me to take time off to write. I could have just stayed in Dumfries, but I chose 'Writing in Interesting Places' as my theme and set off first for New York, then to the Dominican Republic where I stayed with the Scottish writer Alistair Reid for a month. From there I set out for Machu Picchu.

All the time I worked diligently at a journal, first to see how it would turn out, then with a growing sense of commitment. Machu Picchu, the Lost City of the Incas, was the most impressive thing I had ever seen. Writing about it for five hours afterwards in Cuzco, I finished my first three hundred-page notebook and began a second.

The following day, standing in the queue at Cuzco Airport to check in for a flight to the rain forest of south-east Peru, disaster struck. A lapse of concentration and my shoulder bag, with all my writings, camera and films, was stolen. It was the first of three robberies during my South American travels, but easily the most depressing. My initial feelings were of despair and hopelessness. In fact, for the first forty-eight hours in the rain forest, I could equally well have been on the surface of the moon. But the rain forest is a restorative place and I found an inner strength there that surprised me.

After a few days hanging around Cuzco again on the slightest off-chance something might turn up (it did – another robbery!), I set out for Puno and thence to touristless Amantani island on Lake Titicaca, where I would attempt to piece together what I could remember of my journal, and the poems and the play that I had also lost.

The night before I took the train to Puno, I slept poorly. In this extract from *In the Palace of Serpents*, I describe something of what was going through my mind that night. It is in many ways, the sum of any wisdom I have about writing – my answer for all weathers:

In the darkness, I had an image of the loss of my writing. It had to do with height and space. As I wrote my journal, I had felt the thickness of the left-hand side grow pleasantly fat – a

satisfying fertility. I mounted the steps of each morning with a
neat day and date. And then suddenly, it was gone. It was
like diving into a huge space, a timeless space. The past –
where was it? The future – what was the point? It was a
feeling almost of free-falling light-headedness. I was falling,
falling, shouting louder, louder:

> *'Soy escritor*
> *Soy escritor*
> *Soy ESCRITOR.'*

I had never really felt it before or known what it meant.
Usually, I looked sheepish – it is the Scottish way – and
claimed 'to write a bit'. Now, now that all was lost, lost too
was the vanity of the bulging notebook, the diversity of
material, the forward-looking pleasure of unpacking my
treasures and giving them some kind of independent life.
And all that was left was this bloodied, raw desire to write; to
acknowledge, 'this also happened; this also will be written
about'. I saw in my eyes not just the trace of a hunted look,
but a determination: *'Soy escritor'*. Some things you cannot
steal: for five hours I had thought and written about Machu
Picchu at the highest level of my consciousness. And certain
kinds of knowledge you can only find out about one way –
through pain. In this, loving and writing I discovered are
similar pursuits.

> If your love was true
> and you lose it, what have you lost?
> Not the act of loving. That's yours.

> If your words were true
> and you lose them, what have you lost?
> Not the act of writing. That's yours too.

> In loving, in writing, how can you
> hold onto a finished thing? Whether
> you lose it or put it beneath glass

it is the act itself you must cherish.
For what's left, when the moment has passed,
the wind will carry. Despite you.

JOAN LINGARD

Joan Lingard was born in Edinburgh and brought up in Belfast. She has drawn on her knowledge and experience of both cities for her novels, as well as her husband's background in Latvia and Canada. A prolific author of novels for adults and young people, she has three grown-up daughters and one grandson, and lives in Edinburgh with her Canadian husband.

At the 1993 Edinburgh Book Festival she launched two new books, *Night Fires* for young people, and *After Colette*, a novel for adults.

Previous titles include:

The Twelfth Day of July
Across the Barricades
Into Exile
A Proper Place
Hostages to Fortune
The Guilty Party
Frying as Usual
The Freedom Machine

Rags and Riches
Tug of War
The File on Fraulein Berg
Between Two Worlds
Sisters By Rite
The Women's House
The Second Flowering
  of Emily Mountjoy

JOAN LINGARD

Dried Egg and Ketchup

Quite early on I fancied the idea of a literary life. At the age of ten I founded two literary societies, which met in the back yard of my Belfast home. The senior one consisted of myself and my best friend and a girl of eight who was flattered to be invited, and the junior one comprised children all under the age of five. The senior one proved difficult; my best friend and I squabbled endlessly about the form and content of the meetings and folded after a few weeks. The junior club, in contrast, was nothing but a pleasure. The children, whose mothers were no doubt only too happy to be rid of them for a little while, sat amiably cross-legged and uncomplaining on the hard ground while I perched on the coal bunker and read aloud to them from books culled from the narrow dark-brown bookcase in my living-room. They ranged from Marie Corelli to abridged versions of Dickens to Matthew Arnold. I particularly enjoyed reading about Sweetness and Light from Matthew Arnold.

I would like to be able to claim that I was unduly gifted and understood every word I read, but, alas, that was not the case. I was simply bemused by the flow of words, and the longer the sentences and the more obscure the meaning the more I enjoyed myself. I did not consider reading to them from Enid Blyton or Richmal Crompton. Certainly not! I might have the Famous Five and Just William up in my bedroom, but I knew that books such as those were not suitable material for literary societies.

If you are wondering where I got the idea of literary societies from – my parents, although they read books and went to the library, could in no way have been described as 'literary' – the answer is simple: from books. As a child I was an avid reader. I read, and read, and could never get enough to read. I always asked for books for presents and one Christmas received eight, all of which I had read before going to sleep that night. My parents must have found my continual cry of 'I've got nothing to read!' extremely irritating.

The rest of the year I went to the library. Our local children's library, some twenty minutes' walk away, had once been either a shed or a garage; that was the size of it. (The adult library was housed in what had previously been a corner shop and had had its windows painted over.) Most of the books had seen years of service; they'd lost their dust jackets – it was pre-clingfilm days – and been rebound in shades of sludge-brown and dark red in that kind of material that becomes greasy to the touch after much handling. I was a fastidious child and hated the feel of greasy books, so I used to cover them with a brown-paper jacket when I brought them home, just as I did my school books. The pages would also be liberally spattered with splodges of tomato sauce, coffee (Camp) and egg (dried, reconstituted). I was not allowed to bring a book to the table, but it was apparent that numerous children in the district were not similarly restrained. In order not to have to touch the remains of their meals, I would turn the pages over with a slightly stiff white postcard. Through the splats I read Enid Blyton, Arthur Ransome, *The Wind in the Willows*, *Alice in Wonderland*, *What Katy Did*, *Biggles*, *Worrals*, *Pollyanna*, the *Chalet School* stories – more or less everything in the children's library.

One day, when I was eleven years old, and bored, and was delivering my usual moan about lack of reading material into my mother's ear, she, bored with me, turned and said, 'Why don't you go and write a book of your own?' Why not indeed? The suggestion, made, obviously, in desperation, was to affect the course of my life.

I decided to begin straight away. I got lined, foolscap paper, filled my fountain pen with green ink – I thought green would be a desirable, artistic colour for a writer to use – and began to write my first novel. My story concerned a girl called Gail whose parents were removed right at the beginning by the arrival of a telegram summoning them to Rangoon, saying, 'Great-Aunt Emily is ill. Come at once!' I knew that parents would be a nuisance in an adventure story, as they would have a nasty habit of popping up to announce it was bed-time when the heroine was in hot pursuit of a gang of criminals. Also, most books that I'd read did not give too much prominence to parents – children's writers nowadays are more inclined to recognise that parents are rather important in the scheme of things.

Gail goes to stay with her granny in Cornwall. I wouldn't have considered setting my story in Belfast. Dull, deadly old Belfast! You must be joking! What exciting events could ever take place there? It was before the days of the current Troubles, but there were pictures of wanted IRA men outside our local police station, with rewards offered, and I passed every day on my way to school a mural of King Billy in plumed hat, sitting astride his white horse. Not that I could have coped with such topics at the age of eleven. But I had never read a book set in Belfast, did not believe that a house and street such as I lived in, or the people that I knew, could ever be the stuff of fiction. All the books that I wrote as a child and teenager were set in places like the Yorkshire Moors (shades of the Brontës, of course), Applecross (I liked the name), or Rio de Janeiro (ditto). I had never been to any of them, except in my imagination, any more than I had been to Cornwall.

As far as I was concerned, Cornwall was a warren of caves, riddled with secret passages, and hooching with smugglers. So Gail goes exploring and finds a secret passage that leads to a secret cave and then, lo and behold! a villain appears on the scene. He is indisputably a villain since he has a scar on his face that zigzags from the corner of his eye down to the corner of his mouth. Hardly subtle characterisation, but I was, after all, an inexperienced writer. The next development is the fortuitous arrival of Gail's Uncle Bill, a private detective who just happens to have been on the trail of a gang of smugglers for some years, without success. No prizes for guessing what happens or whose influence I was under at the time!

When I had written THE END, with a considerable amount of relish, I looked at the foolscap pages covered with green ink and was not entirely satisfied. I wanted to produce a *book*, to be a proper author, so I procured a hard-backed notebook and copied the whole story out again in my very best writing, using blue ink this time, thinking it unlikely anyone would publish in green; and I had no black. I then made a dust jacket, drawing Gail in Cornwall on the front, giving her long, blonde plaits. A certain amount of wish fulfilment was undoubtedly involved in that, as I longed to grow my hair long and my mother always used to have it cut off in a kind of pudding-bowl style on the grounds that otherwise I might get 'things' in it at school. I wrote the blurb on the inside flap of the jacket, and on the back I put at the top: BOOKS BY JOAN LINGARD. Down the side I wrote the numbers 1 to 24, that being all I could squash in. Opposite number 1, I wrote the rather pathetic title of *Gail*. (I would like to think that my titles have improved with the years.) At the foot of the page I printed: PUBLISHED BY LINGARD AND COMPANY.

From then on I wanted to be a novelist, and nothing else. Not for me short stories or poems, although I enjoyed reading them, and still do. But I liked the length and breadth of the novel, its multi-layered texture, the opportunity to spend a considerable passage of time with the characters, to become intimate with them, and to be absorbed into their different worlds. In my imagination I could share a dormitory with Jo at the Chalet School, fly on missions with Biggles, dive off the cliffs at Acapulco with Richard Haliburton, explore the outback of Australia and the wilds of Canada. And I find that, when I travel to places such as Florence, Paris, New York, San Francisco, Sydney, the echoes of recognition that I pick up come from books – mostly novels – read over the years.

I am as avid a reader now as I was at the age of eleven, though I could no longer manage to read eight books in a day! And I fortunately no longer have to turn pages with a postcard and read through splats of dried egg and ketchup. One of my greatest pleasures is to anticipate the opening of a brand-new, unstained hardback book.

Into Print

" Thank you for your
letter of rejection. I find it
rather unsatisfactory and
lacking the style & substance
we're looking for at this time.
We receive many such
letters and I'm afraid yours
is typical
of the
sloppy etc
etc
etc "

Calman

Illustration by Mel Calman

MAEVE BINCHY

(Photo: Liam White)

Maeve Binchy was born in 1940 in Co. Dublin, the eldest of a happy middle-class family, and went to a convent school in nearby Killiney. She studied History and French at University College, Dublin, taught for eight years in girls' schools, then joined the *Irish Times* as a columnist in 1968.

She began to write fiction after she met her husband, the British writer and broadcaster Gordon Snell. Her first venture into book publishing came when her journalistic writing was collected in two volumes. These were followed by four books of short stories and four plays, two each for stage and television. But it was when she began writing novels that Maeve Binchy's career took off, with sensational sales in twelve languages all over the world. Two of her novels have been televised.

Previous titles include:

Light a Penny Candle	*Firefly Summer*
London Transports	*Silver Wedding*
Echoes	*Circle of Friends*
The Lilac Bus	*The Copper Beech*

MAEVE BINCHY

Just Mention Me in the Acknowledgments

When I was a fat little girl in a green school uniform I was dying to be famous.

It looked like a difficult journey to get there. I was no good at games. I couldn't sing or play the piano, I got red and confused when I tried to recite in public, I was too afraid of martyrdom to be a proper saint.

When I was nine, I won a competition in a missionary magazine writing a story about how a poisonous girl called Jane went to Black Africa and stopped everyone doing what they were doing and converted them to being Catholics. My name was in the magazine so I was a bit famous, but it was too goody-goody and didn't count.

When I was twenty-three I went to work in a kibbutz in Israel where mercifully I didn't try to stop them doing what they were doing, but to stop my mother worrying about me I wrote long letters home telling them more or less what I was up to and how a kibbutz worked.

My parents thought all their geese were swans. They thought my account was brilliant and typed it out and sent it to a newspaper. When I got back I was a bit more famous because of that and also without knowing it I had actually found the voice with which I have written since – the voice of total simplicity as if I were talking to friends . . . which was what I *had* been doing. I wrote to my parents without seeking a style, without polishing a sentence and with no intention to impress. All I was trying to do was to tell them what it was like in a strange hot land, where people worked cheerfully in the desert, where we ate oranges and did guard duty, where nobody went to Mass or cared what neighbours might be saying. Where they gave their children to be looked after in children's houses even though it broke their hearts. All I was trying to do was to paint the picture.

But the best of lessons are often not learned because we think they are too simple.

I didn't realise at once that this was the way I should write, in sentences without any hidden agenda, in words that would build up an image of the place rather than roll off the tongue when read aloud.

I thought writing was Prose.

And that Prose was a Big Deal.

So buoyed up by this publication of my insights into the economy of the Negev and the fact that it been considered good enough to appear in a national newspaper, I wrote on vainly with pretensions tumbling over pomposity, and one by one every article or story that I sent out was returned to me. It was a huge mystery at the time. If I had done so well and gained instant recognition when I was *not* trying, I thought I should have done twenty times better when I *was* trying.

It took a few years to realise that in the very trying I was losing whatever spontaneity and freshness I had in the first place. The way I was tarting up my ideas and trying to make them sound sophisticated just rendered them a bag of clichés and imitations. So one day I cut free: I wrote a piece about school, I wrote that I, as a teacher, often knew more about the girls who sat in front of me every day for six years than did their parents. I knew when they were having rows, or friendships had ended, I knew when they were bursting with idealism and hope for the world, I knew when they hated the way they looked and crouched and sulked because they thought the rest of the world was beautiful and they were the only ugly flowers in the garden. There were no educational theories in this piece, no statistics, nothing that would impress anyone. Yet it was published at once, and hailed as the kind of view that would revolutionise education. A teacher that cared, and wished that a lot of the parents cared more.

Of course, like everyone with over-ambitious hopes about being famous and having something to say, I had tried writing fiction but I had never dared to show it to anyone, and once I realised with a blinding glimpse into the obvious that you were more honest and believable if you spoke as yourself instead of as an amalgam of everyone else you had admired or been jealous of . . . I looked at that fiction again.

It was unreadable.

Even by the one who had written it.

So, wincing with embarrassment, I put it away and tried to write as I spoke, telling the kind of tale I would tell to a friend, putting in the depth of feeling that I had myself, not more and not less. There would be no artistic spare understatement in my writing. That's not the kind of person I am. I am large, exuberant, good-natured, speak very quickly, I am full of enthusiasms, and would prefer to deliver myself of a lot of opinions that some might find either unacceptable or simplistic than to deliver myself of monosyllables or enigmatic pauses.

So I invented heroines who were a bit like myself, with problems such as those that had confronted me, and the people I knew. I wrote and wrote, a huge long novel. Because I take so long to get to the point, I had done four hundred pages before anyone got to the age of puberty so the main events of the book were somewhat delayed. I unwillingly cut out about three hundred pages of childhood and went at it again.

And that was the first of many novels which took off like I had never dreamed they would. They have been translated into languages that still astound me. What do Koreans or Finns or Israelis make of these people I have written about? Sometimes they write to me and say that my childhood must have been just like theirs. Or that they had loved a man like Johnny Stone or been a friend of a girl like Benny Hogan.

It is, of course, hugely satisfying. I would be mad if I didn't admit that. And I suppose I realise a bit why people believe the stories. They are not about real people – my father, a lawyer, warned me so much about that and the dread of libel actions hung so heavily over me that I wouldn't put a hint of a real person into a book.

But they are honest and truthful in that I have banished the pretentious side of myself and I write only what I know to be true as I see it. I have always known that children are both proud of their families and ashamed of them at the same time – the two things go hand in hand. So that's the way I write it. I have never known a person to be so bad that there isn't some redeeming feature, or so good and loved that there can't be an irritating factor to be found in them as well.

In my heart I'm still a teacher, I want to share whatever I know. It gives me a great buzz to think I could pass on some hint or bit of advice that worked for me anyway. I don't want you to dedicate your whole book to me, if this works for you. Just mention me in the acknowledgments. That will be satisfaction enough.

RICHARD FORD

(Photo: Sally Soames)

Richard Ford was born in Jackson, Mississippi, in 1944. He attended Michigan State University, Washington University Law School and the University of California. He began writing short stories at the age of twenty-four. His first novel, *A Piece of My Heart*, was runner-up for the Ernest Hemingway Award. He has lived throughout the United States and has taught at Princeton University, Williams College and the University of Michigan.

Previous titles include:

A Piece of My Heart *The Sportswriter*
Rock Springs *Wildlife*
The Ultimate Good Luck

RICHARD FORD

The Beginning, as Viewed from the Middle

At my particular age, forty-eight (neither exactly young nor exactly old is how that feels), most partisan arguments aimed at proving some general truth about the world resolve themselves – in my mind anyway – into what I think of as nice, existential equilibrium: almost nothing seems to be generally true, almost nothing generally false, so that the best anyone can do is find his own way, reveal it as such, and go on hopefully. Counsel, real counsel, in the way Walter Benjamin meant it – useful words about human life – is and always has been very hard to come by. Benjamin believed counsel was the great virtue of told stories, those spoken in the human voice by wise travellers, and that in them the righteous man might encounter himself in the person of the storyteller.

Which was all very well when we had plenty of those tellers, whose faces we knew, out and around visiting homes without TVs, where people passed their evenings weaving and spinning. Now storytelling itself is a brisk cottage industry. Slews of young writers stay up nights, letting no one in, trying their best to write well and be read, at a time when books are popularly conceived as cordless mini-series, and getting read is hard. Both giving and taking counsel require adapting, I guess. The human voice must be listened for more freely and also more acutely. The righteous man, *whoever he is*, needs to take consolation more willingly, and be ready to encounter himself less in the person of the storyteller or even in the tale told properly, and more in the fabric of a life which might simply be like his. After all, even Benjamin admits that counsel is 'less an answer to a question than a proposal concerning the continuation of a story which is just unfolding'.

When I got out of school, in 1970, ready to begin being a writer, there seemed to hold sway in my country a kind of conventional wisdom regarding writing, and particularly getting started writing; a protocol for getting work (stories, in my case) published into the world and eventually read by real readers.* I'm no longer sure that such a protocol exists in the minds of young American writers today. I do not even know why we thought what *we* thought. But we thought it, acted on it. And for some people it worked out fine, while for others – me – it didn't.

Wisdom was, that for young writers there was a particular 'publishing world' out there in America, a world divided into hemispheres. One hemisphere was the sub-world of small presses, literary magazines, university reviews. And the other, more brilliant upper half was the world of large-circulation, widely read, money-paying, famous-making magazines printed on slick pages, and not in Baton Rouge or Bowling Green, but in New York and Boston. The Big Time this was.

What we – or at least I – understood about this whole world was that I needed to 'break into it'. There was a 'level' I could empirically find by sending my stories out – literary magazines were where one started – and either getting them back or having them approved or published. Good stories were to be found there, it was alleged, and mine would stand a chance. Once I'd done that, broken into print, I could try to 'move up' to better, more widely read and distributed magazines – there was a floating sense of which were better than others. My work, my name would begin to get around. I would see some action. Acceptance would be a word I'd hear more. Money would rarely change hands, but I was not in

---

*Readers are people you don't know or aren't related to.

this for money (and, truly, I wasn't). All this would go along for a while, years perhaps, while I got better, while I had more work published, while my name on a manuscript began to be associated with good writing; until, by some act of providence, a story of mine would get 'taken' upwards by an editor from another world, the one where all the bright lights were turned on. And then I would be someplace. That would be the *it* heard in the phrase 'You've made *it*'.

The trouble was, this progression didn't work for me. Oh, it worked for others well enough. Some of the finest, most admirable writers writing today have gone up through these ranks, their good stories published, their readership solidly banked by their earliest admirers. And some writers, of course, simply ignored this whole ladder-and-rung business altogether, sent stories to the *New Yorker* or the *Atlantic*, got the good word straight away, hit the ground running, and have never looked back. Much maligned now by spoilsports, such early and great success must've been very sweet. I'd have handled mine admirably, I'm sure. In any case, all formulas for creating one's writing life break down once the first term – *I write a story* – is put into place.

I, however, could not get my stories published. I sent them to many – very many – of the magazines that were on everyone's checklist. (Actual mimeographed lists were eventually compiled by who-knows-what mysterious samaritan using the *Writer's Digest* and some unverifiable word-of-mouth about publications generously, if inexplicably, courting unpublished writers.) I kept a log, a little notebook in which I had lined off little boxes, inside which I wrote where this story was sent when, and when it came back, where it went next. Somebody – I forget who now – told me this is what I should do. I needed to be orderly. Systematic. It was serious business I was up to. The strangling horror that a story would be accepted at two or perhaps three magazines at once, the embarrassment, and bad editorial blood this would cause to flow, could all be avoided this way. Meanwhile, the system, my logging in dates and destinations like a shipping clerk, would give me something to do while I awaited my own good news, offer solace when there wasn't good news. And there wasn't.

I was persistent. I kept my stories out. I furrowed my brows over levels. Maybe the *Cimarron Review* in faraway Oklahoma was just too good for me at this point; I should send a story to a magazine with a less resolute name. I remember one called *Fur-Bearing Trout*, published who knows where, maybe Minnesota, but where I was chattily turned down by an editor who said he didn't like short stories longer than eight pages, though they need not be about fish.

I pulled strings – any ones I thought I had. To *Sumac*, a magazine in Michigan, I wrote that I was a graduate of Michigan State. That seemed cagey. To a magazine in Mississippi, I bragged I was a native. No dice. I got my friend whom the *Cimarron Review* firmly admired and regularly published to recommend me. No again. I even got an old teacher who had once taught Willie Morris, then the editor of *Harper's*, to middleman a story to that esteemed magazine – shooting, just once, for the moon. No.

Once a man named Nick Crome (I hope he's happy, wherever he is) asked me to revise a story I'd sent to his magazine, *TransPacific*, published in of all places, Colorado. Though when I eagerly did and returned it to him, he ignored my new version, but asked me to badger my local library (which happened to be the Chicago Public Library) into subscribing and inserting his magazine on to its shelves. I admit it – I wrote him promptly and suggested where he ought best insert his magazine, whereupon he dispatched to me a three-page, single-spaced letter full of invective and threat in which he periodically used the red half of his ribbon for emphasis, and in which he called me 'sonny', 'sport', 'ace', 'junior', a 'simpleton', a 'sorry, petulant fool', and an 'ignorant motherfucker'. To his credit, though, he also wrote this to me: 'I devote most of my waking hours to the attempt to promote the careers of people like you, ace. I do this not only by publishing them – but by writing every one personally, so they know there's a real person here, who knows who they are and who does read what they write . . . My wife, who is now acting as business manager, tells me you're not a subscriber. That's okay – relatively few care about preserving the means by which young writers in

America find publication – shit, junior, they just want to get PUBLISHED!!!!!' 'Published' was one of those words typed in red.

Seasoning, I think this is called. Dues paying. Learning the ropes. Getting my feet wet. Starting at the bottom. I was doing this. Only nobody liked my stories.

Finally a call came from a friend in California. A magazine, he said, in New Zealand was interested in new American writing. Maybe I could send something there. New Zealand, I thought, gazing out my window at an unpromising winter sky. A nice place. English spoken there. New Zealand. Yes. I would. And sure enough the editors took my story, even asked for another, which I sent and they agreed to publish soon. For a time in the winter of 1971, I thought very, very fondly about New Zealand, about what good people were there. Readers. People willing to give you a chance. Careless of trends, vogues, reputations. It was summer there, then. I thought of Mr Peggotty in *David Copperfield*, sailing off to Australia, which was near New Zealand: 'We will begin a new life over there,' is how he put it. Exuberant. Valiant. I considered a move.

First, though, I fastidiously entered the titles of my two stories and their new homes into my logbook beside the word 'accepted', and into the heretofore empty space on my curriculum vitae reserved for publications. New Zealand. It seemed farther away there on that page than when the happy letters had arrived. I wondered for a moment what someone would think who saw these entries, what sort of writer they'd think I was, what form of giggly desperation inhabited me that I needed to send my stories all the way down there. Would they realise that North American serial rights for each story were still intact, and I could still publish the stories stateside if I wanted to? And who would ever read these stories? The editors – all good fellows – liked them, paid them compliments. But no one else ever weighed in with praise or complaint or notice of any kind. All was quiet. And in a month I decided not to move to New Zealand. Not yet. It wasn't going anyplace, after all. Though neither was I.

I went back to circulating my stories. *Epoch, North American Review, Red Clay Reader, New American Review* – all famous literary magazines where I'd read some writers whose names I knew. Philip Roth, William Gass, Robert Coover. I quit writing cagey cover letters. My own 'production', however, was beginning to slow. I'd written eight or so stories, I was twenty-seven years old, and I felt I was becoming confused about my 'style'. My logbook was filled up. A student journal at a small Ohio college agreed to print a story, but one I'd written three years ago – when I was just starting school! The editor loved it: 'If you can write like this,' I remember his letter saying, 'you should be writing for the *slicks*.' Only I couldn't write like that anymore. I'd 'developed' beyond this. Maybe I shouldn't have. What did he know?

It all got me down. That much I can tell you. Stories would whistle back into my mailbox just ahead of a dark mistral. I'd read the enclosed letters, check to see if the story was still clean and enough undented by paper clips to send out again, gulp down some unbearable bitterness, and then just quit for the day. Usually I'd have a drink about 10.45 in the morning and take a long walk until my wife got off work and there was something new to take heart from.

And then, unsuddenly, I quit writing stories, 'gagged by the silence of others', as Sartre says. I was discouraged. But I do not think I was disillusioned. Even then I knew that a life, even a short one like mine, dedicated to literature was not a wasted life. I was merely a failure at what I was doing, and along with failure's other dull commissions comes – as should be – the opportunity to think things over. Failure may not always inspire one's best decisions, but one's profoundest convictions do often arise nearby.

And so, in the late winter of 1971, in Chicago, I took an account of the world and, as it says in Dickens, my 'personal history, adventures, experience and observation' of it.

There is a koan often overheard among avant-gardists and inside the better, more progressive American graduate writing programmes, which asks: is it not almost always the case that you can tell a good story by that fact that very few people like it? Considering, however, who were the few who liked my stories, I did not feel I had the full comfort of even that befuddling wisdom. And, in any case, I *wanted* people to like my stories. More importantly, I wanted people to *read* them, even if they couldn't like them. I believed – or I came to believe that winter – that writers, the ones I cared about, wrote to be read; not to aggrandise themselves in cringing élitism, not to please or psychoanalyse themselves by getting closer to their feelings, and not, indeed, just to be published and to fill that empty space on a résumé. Writers wrote, I concluded, not even to appeal to a particular readership, but to discover and bring to precious language the most important things they were capable of, and to reveal this to others with the hope that it will have an effect on them – please them, teach them, console them. Reach them.

I, it was plain, wasn't succeeding here. Nobody was reading my stories because, I decided, they simply weren't very good – not good enough, anyway. Maybe I knew it in my back-brain; maybe I just trusted the editors who sent them all back to me. But I knew it. It's true I've always trusted rejection more than acceptance (at the time I'd had more experience with rejection). But it's also true that I came to believe that no good writer would go unpublished. Perhaps this was just the original, free, and blind act of writer's faith, but if so, it seemed to me collateralised by the lavish evidence of so much awful writing – even if not mine – routinely finding its 'home' in print.

Beyond these first principles of belief, certain practical matters became apparent to me. I did not write very fast. I wrote hard; but at my pace I would never get the proper amount of low-level publishing experience to move up through the ranks. Too few at-bats, we say here. Moreover, I didn't like the whole major league/minor league premise of that conventional wisdom I'd inherited. I read the magazines I'd been submitting to, as well as the ones I wished I could, and I couldn't see evidence that the premise worked very well. Plenty of terrible stories were popping up in both leagues. There was reason to believe, in fact, that not a whole lot of really excellent writing got done, or probably ever did. That, of course, is still the case, though it doesn't discourage anyone, nor should it.

Even more to the point, I began to resent what seemed to me the unprovable premise that there existed *any* useful structure or scheme of ascendable rungs whose rule was that my stories weren't good enough at first but might be better later on; and that I should have patience and go on surrendering myself to its clankings. What I felt was that I wanted my stories to be great stories, as good as could be written. And now. And if they weren't (and they weren't) that was my own business, my problem, not the concern of some system for orderly advancement in the literary arts, some wisdom kept presumptuously active by wretched, grad-student magisters sitting before piles of manuscripts, or else some already belly-up writer who'd changed boats middle-course and fallen into being an 'editor'. I had hard thoughts that winter. But I meant my failings to be my own affair.

Some people, I guess, thrive by deferring to unknown and presumably higher authority, to the benevolence of vast, indistinct institutions. And, of course, it's never a simple matter when your whole life requires submitting your efforts and yourself continually to the judgment of others. We all accommodate that. But most of the writers I have respected and still respect seem to me not so adept at discerning and respecting underlying design, but at trying to invent designs anew. What was out there, I thought eighteen years ago, and think even more this minute, is not a structure for writers to surrender to, but fidgety, dodgy chaos. And our privileged task is to force it, calm it to our wills.

What I did then, with all this fresh in mind, was put my stories away in their tabbed folders, fattened by the various drafts and revisions and rejection notices that lodged with them, and dedicate myself to writing a novel, which I assumed would take years, and did. Not that I propose this strategy for anyone else. My belief about starting novels, and particularly the first one, is that you treat the impulse like the impulse to marry: solemnly, and with the proviso that if you can talk yourself out of it you should. If you can't, then there's no advice to give you.

But I needed to get better – much, much better at what I was doing, and in ways I don't even want to think about now. A novel would take those years; I could go more slowly; there was more to work on, get better at. No demoralising rejections would crash into my mailbox every morning. One might eventually come, but it was far off. And in trade for this easement, this slow-going, this sumptuous usage of my time and youth, I'd have a novel, maybe, when all was over – a not inconsiderable achievement. It was a bargain I was only too happy to enter.

Thinking back on 1971, I am even more convinced now than I could've been then. Not that a commanding philosophy of the writer's life was forged on this one decision. I still want my work published – that was the only way it would ever get read. This was simply a matter of practical protocol: I decided I could do my best *at a distance* from the preoccupations and the institutions and the thin solace and the misfires of publication. Said another way, failure at publishing stories where I wanted and tried vigorously to publish them turned me back to my work, which is what's important. 'Success', which I still calibrate in readers, was withheld, and I somehow was encouraged – even if it felt different at the time.

I dignify my decision now by believing that publication of those first stories might've just plain shot me in the foot by conferring approval – of some kind – on work I wanted to be good but that wasn't very good. When I look around in literary bookstores now, and in the back ad pages of magazines, it seems that with patience and resourcefulness *every* writer can find a publisher for everything that's written – good, bad, mediocre. And while I won't wag a finger at publishing too fast – or publishing your buddies or publishing the famous because they're thought to be 'lightning rods of the culture' (as a famous editor recently admitted) or even just publishing a magazine that nobody but the editors and their parents will ever read – I have now written enough stories myself that 'aren't right for us' or that 'would surely find a home elsewhere' so as to feel sovereignty over this one opinion: publishing work that's no good probably isn't a very good idea for writers and publishers, either one, no matter where along the literary ladder they happen to be clinging. For writers, it's hard when no one likes your work, and hard in another way when things begin finally to break for you; but it's best to try and set your own high standards for what's good and what isn't – even if, God knows, you happen to have written the stuff yourself.

Finally, small presses, literary magazines, university reviews do still have a place in my writing life. On occasion they have been willing to publish what – by my own standards – have been stories as good as I can write after years of trying. I do not, however, believe that small presses or literary journals are 'where it's at' for writing in my country, any more than I believe the *New Yorker* or *Esquire* or *Granta* are more perceptive or appreciative or forgiving than other putative audiences, or that their editors are any more open-minded, generally willing to take risks, less capricious, less victims of cronyism, or had their ears more finely tuned to excellent writing than anybody else who sets up as a public literary arbiter. True, those slick magazines are run to the tune of profits. But one fellow's profit is likely to be another man's principle. Who's to say whose god is meaner, coarser?

Where it's *at* for literature in my country is where it's always been – with writers, and what they write. Writing is dark and lonely work, and no one has to do it, and no one will even care if it doesn't get done at all, so that choosing to do it and trying to do it well is enough of an existential errand, enough of a first step, and for whatever my money and counsel's worth, enough of a last step too.

ALLAN MASSIE

Born in Singapore in 1938, Allan Massie was brought up in Aberdeenshire and read history at Trinity College, Cambridge. To date, he has written eleven novels, including *A Question of Loyalties* which won the Saltire Society Book of the Year Award. His non-fiction titles include a study of Muriel Spark and an historical work on the twelve emperors of Ancient Rome.

Allan Massie is a Fellow of the Royal Society of Literature and has been a Booker Prize judge. He is the *Scotsman*'s lead fiction reviewer and writes regularly for the *Daily Telegraph*. He lives in the Borders with his wife and three children.

Previous titles include:

Change and Decay in
   All Around I See
The Last Peacock
The Death of Men
One Night in Winter
Augustus

A Question of Loyalties
The Hanging Tree
The Sins of the Father
Tiberius
Caesar
These Enchanted Woods

ALLAN MASSIE

First Steps

I was in my early thirties and had published nothing. There had been attempts, sad things, I'm afraid. I recall a rather embarrassing ghost story, submitted to *Blackwood's Magazine*, and politely, but mercifully, rejected. There were some 20,000 words perhaps of a Jacobite novel, a long way, leagues and leagues, after Stevenson. It may be about somewhere; I trust it never surfaces. There were other stories and bits and pieces, all influenced by whomever I had been reading most recently. Once in a bar in Rome near the Pantheon, I showed something I had written to an English journalist I used to meet there with his girlfriend, a Polish violinist with a fine downy moustache. (She gave me incidentally a beautiful first line for a novel, but I haven't used it yet, though I hope some day to do so.) Antony read what I offered. 'Can't you write anything that's your own?' he said. A sound judgment, but painful at the time.

Then it happened that I was out of work and in a bad way in several ways. So, to salvage self-esteem, I took to writing. As Johnson said of Richard Savage: 'Having no profession, he became by necessity an author'. I started a novel; fortunately, I also wrote some short stories.

I sent one to the *London Magazine*. Even then, more than twenty years ago, there were few outlets for the short story, but I cannot remember why I chose to send it there. I doubt if

I had seen the *London Magazine* for several years, and I knew its editor Alan Ross only as *The Observer's* cricket correspondent. I think that first story came back. If it's the one I am thinking of, it deserved to come back. It was a boxing story, and the rhythms, if nothing else, were Hemingway's. But the postcard that accompanied the rejection – Ross has always communicated by postcards, sometimes featuring steeplechasers he has owned – offered just a hint that he would like to see something else.

That was enough, encouragement enough. Soon, there was a story beginning:

'What are you doing down there, Uncle Tom?'
The man lying on the bathroom floor opened his eyes. He saw the lapis-lazuli tiles, the crimson bath-mat and then immediately over him, casting a shadow, the sturdy widespread legs. 'Ssh,' he said.

Off it went. A postcard returned: 'Like the story. Can you let me know something about yourself?'

Like Muriel Spark's Fleur Talbot (a few years later, actually), I went on my way rejoicing.

He took other stories subsequently, gave me books to review, and told me to fine myself for any echo of Hemingway. It was some months before that first story came out, in an edition devoted to 'New Writers, New Stories' – one of the other new writers was David Pownall – but that didn't matter. I was on my way, a justified sinner.

I owe a lot to Ross, and am conscious that it is a debt which cannot be paid and which more reprehensibly I have perhaps never tried to pay. For almost thirty years now he has been running the best literary magazine in Britain, quirky, sometimes eccentric, but always readable and usually distinguished. He has done it with little help and sometimes only with the company of a Border collie. He has encouraged young writers as well as his contemporaries, especially those among them like Peter Vansittart who have never had the commercial success their work merits. He has given a home to short stories and confidence to their authors. Graham Swift, William Boyd and Helen Harris are three whom he was the first, or among the first, to publish. There are countless others. Established writers have never been excluded but they have never been the point of the magazine. Every issue has borne the mark of his own personality and taste, and yet few magazines have been less egocentric. He has been committed only to the cause of good writing; bless him.

Soon after he took that first story, I had my second stroke of luck. Robert Nye reviewed a biography of Scott Fitzgerald in the *Scotsman*, and since I was very keen on Fitzgerald at the time and didn't altogether agree with Mr Nye's point of view, I wrote to him to say so. I did this with some trepidation because, so magisterial was his manner, I thought he was at least twenty years older than myself, and so it seemed rather cheek on my part. (He is in fact a few months younger.) At any rate he replied, at some length and with what I now know to be characteristic generosity. And he ended his letter ended his letter with the question: 'Are you a writer or something?' Thanks to Ross, I was able to summon the audacity to reply that I was indeed a writer.

We continued to correspond – I was by now living in Italy. He introduced me to Willis Pickard, then Literary Editor of the *Scotsman*, and this opened the door to journalism. Our friendship flourished, even after we met. Often such meetings are disappointing and writers are wiser to restrict relationships to correspondence; but not this time. I received encouragement and good advice from him, as from Ross.

Encouragement and good advice are what aspirant writers most need, and I was fortunate to find two such mentors and friends. Without them, who knows what would have become of me?

In Spite Of

Illustration by Anthony Browne

SARA PARETSKY

The daughter of two academics, Sara Paretsky was born and brought up in Kansas. She moved to Chicago in 1969, with a degree in Political Science. She has worked as a conference manager, freelance business manager for a large insurance company, as well as acquiring an MBA, and a PhD on the English Civil War. She and her husband, an English professor of physics, live in a Victorian house in Chicago's south-east side.

Voted 1987 Woman of the Year by *Ms* magazine, Sara Paretsky is one of the founders of Sisters in Crime, and the author of seven V. I. Warshawski novels. Her fifth novel, *Toxic Shock*, won the 1988 Crime Writers' Association Silver Dagger Award.

Previous titles include:

Deadlock	*Toxic Shock*
Killing Order	*Burn Marks*
Indemnity Only	*Guardian Angel*
Bitter Medicine	*A Woman's Eye* (Ed.)

SARA PARETSKY

Journeying Together

I felt at a loss when Jenny Brown told me she wanted me to talk about writing – about how I write, or how I came to write, or some combination of the two. I give a lot of public lectures, but I shy away from talking about my own work, whether about its content or about how I do it. And that's because I really don't know how to write – I don't know *how* I do what I do. I've never had any formal training as a writer. And I'm afraid if I tinker with the mechanism too much – either by thinking or talking about it – my writing will leave me as mysteriously as it came.

My husband is a thorough-going WASP. On top of that he's a scientist, a physicist, so neither by birth nor by training can he have any empathy with the mind of a Polish peasant who fears the Evil Eye. But that's me, or a part of me. One of my grandmothers came actually not from Poland but from modern-day Lithuania. (In her day it was Russian, then it became briefly Polish, then was divided between the Germans and the Russians in the von Ribbentrop–Molotov Pact, then became Russian again, and now is trying to be just Lithuania.)

Be that as it may, it was from this grandmother that I learned of the Evil Eye which would infallibly pounce on me – if I bragged too much about my looks, or any possible talent I might possess, or later on, talents possessed by my stepsons. She also taught me never to say *Gesundheit* to someone who was coughing because it would make them have a coughing fit and die. And she said never, ever give a pregnant woman a baby shower because that would kill her unborn child.

Perhaps it is this belief that we all have the power to kill others by the mere utterance of a word, or the giving of a shower, that prompted me to write murder mysteries.

At any rate, instead of bringing the Evil Eye down on myself by telling you how I write, let me describe a bit of the circuitous path I followed to become not a writer, but a published writer.

As I was thinking about what I might say I came on John Updike's front-page essay in the 5 August 1990 *New York Times* book review. In it he described his depression and the end of Rabbit, as well as how he came to write the first Rabbit novel, thirty-three years ago, in a small town in Massachusetts. He'd moved to Ipswich, he says, 'in an attempt to get away from the charms and distractions of New York City. . . . I had had a job in New York, I had done my New York thing, I could tell Uptown from Downtown, I had undergone the Manhattan initiation rites that writers should undergo.'

I read this passage and I thought, maybe that's what's wrong with me. Or perhaps not *wrong*, but maybe that's what keeps me from feeling connected to the world of real writers. Because I hadn't undergone the Manhattan initiation rites that writers should undergo.

But then I realised that strictly speaking, even that isn't true. Twenty-one years ago this summer I moved to New York, hoping to become a writer. It had been driven into my unconscious from childhood on, as it apparently was into Updike's, that to be a writer meant moving to New York.

Now I had no money. I wasn't planning to go there to create a novel – I didn't have such grandiose dreams. But I thought in a rather simple-minded way that I could show the *New Yorker*, or *New York*, or *Harper's*, or the dailies, or any of the thousand magazines and papers published there, examples of my writing – all unpublished – history essays and short stories (what a portfolio!) and that one of these publications might take me on in some very junior capacity.

So armed with a two hundred-dollar loan from a friend, which twenty years ago was enough to live on in New York for a few weeks, I made the rounds but never got past the front desk. I had no contacts. I was so ignorant I didn't know you needed a sponsor to get into one of those places. And even if I'd known that, I wouldn't have been able to figure out how to find one. It's possible, too, that my skills are not now and weren't then, suited for journalism, but I never got far enough in the process to have them evaluated.

As my two weeks' grace drew to a close and I began to panic about what I might live on, I fulfilled my destiny. I became a secretary. After four months I decided to return to Chicago. I could be a secretary there just as easily, and Chicago offered certain advantages over New York. For instance, in Chicago when you picked up the phone to make a call you could count on getting a dial tone. In New York at that time you might wait up to half an hour for one. Given the rate of forcible break-ins in the part of the Upper West Side where I found an apartment to share, a dial tone seemed like a necessity, not a luxury. I realise that a real writer would not have been deterred by such pedestrian considerations, and it adds to my sense of unease in discussing my work.

I should point out in passing that when my agent sent out my first book, *Indemnity Only*, eleven years ago, a lot of editors turned it down because of the Chicago setting. They didn't think PI novels worked outside of LA or New York. In fact, they didn't think people read outside of LA or New York. Perhaps they imagined that in Chicago – because we could get dial tones – we spent all our time on the phone.

When I say I fulfilled my destiny in becoming a secretary, I refer to the external expectations for my life in the milieu in which I was raised. I grew up in Kansas in the golden age of America, in a society where everyone had a defined place, where everyone knew right from wrong – and what happened when you forgot.

We had mandatory prayer (Protestant) in our public schools. The same schools barred blacks from college track courses. In those golden days they knew better than to agitate about it. Abortion was a crime (as it is rapidly becoming again). Only bad girls had sex outside marriage –

whereupon they reaped their inevitable punishment since such contraceptives as existed weren't available to unmarried women.

Best of all, we little girls knew we were destined to be mommies. We didn't worry about careers. Except for some married teachers, secretaries and waitresses, the only women who worked were those too strange or too unfortunate – in our eyes – to get husbands.

Our dreams were of our weddings. When Roxanne Farrell 'had to get married' in our sophomore year of high school, to us the most tawdry part was that she bought her trousseau at Woolworths. Good girls who waited until they graduated from high school or college bought fancy bridalwear at the Plaza in Kansas City.

Male writers such as Sartre and Bellow have recorded knowing early in life that their destiny lay in literature. Bellow knew he was 'born to be a performing and interpretive creature', Sartre that he was born for words.

I call myself a writer, but feebly, without conviction. Where did they get this sense, I wonder? Were their childhoods spent like mine? I wrote from an early age, but I knew that as in all fields literature belonged to men. The history and biography we studied in school told tales of the deeds of men. We learned to speak of the aspirations of mankind and of 'man's inhumanity to man', his inhumanity to women not being worth recording.

And the literature we studied was all written by men. If they were like me, Bellow and Sartre may not even have known that women wrote in a serious way, that the first novelist to treat psychology as a significant force in human lives was a woman. Sartre's boyhood was spent with Flaubert, Cornelius, Homer, Shakespeare. Bellow turned to Anderson, Dreiser, Edgar Lee Masters, Vachel Lindsay.

The books Sartre's grandmother read were feminine, he says, and he was taught by his grandfather to deem them inferior. By an odd chance I learned the same lesson. We studied only one novel by a woman in my school – and her first name was George. Although I wept over *Little Women*, the moral of Jo March's life is that little girls must put aside the dream of literature to perform the higher duty of looking after their families.

Did Jean-Paul or Saul's childhood resemble mine in other ways? Was their first responsibility to look after the little children – to spend summer vacation and evenings after school taking them for walks, changing their diapers, feeding them, cleaning their rooms, reading them their stories? Did their fathers tell them their works were derivative, that they lacked the genius necessary for originality? Did their mothers assure them that the work their sisters did was superior to anything they could ever achieve, that the future lies with girls, not boys? Can destiny swim in such waters?

The messages that I got at home were invidious and insistent: that my words might be amusing, even entertaining, but they were not original or worth pursuing. In fact, the only story I ever tried to make public was one I wrote at the age of thirteen for a national competition sponsored by the *Atlantic* magazine.

My father read it after I submitted it. He told me that the story was so derivative that the magazine would no doubt think I had plagiarised it, and not to be surprised when it didn't win a prize. With all the earnestness of my age, and of my personality, I wrote to the magazine explaining what he had said, and assuring them that it was my own work, that if it resembled someone else's story it wasn't done on purpose. When I told my father what I'd done, thinking he'd be relieved that I'd owned up to the problem, he became furious in the frightening way that only a very violent person can become. So it's perhaps not surprising that I waited another twenty years before trying to publish anything else.

Anyway, when I was sixteen, my parents sent me through a secretarial course so that if I didn't marry right after college I would be able to support myself. Even in 1963 there were other career alternatives for women.

I have a great deal of respect for good secretaries. And I know from intimate experience what the frustrations of their jobs entail. But the twin futures of wife and secretary should not be the limiting horizons of a girl's life as they were of mine. Even now, with six published novels behind me, and a seventh on the way, I sit and sweat every time I try to write, and wonder, am I doing it right? If it fails – if I fail, if I've lost that something, that thing I can't define that enables me to tell stories that other people want to read – what will I do? And my first thought is always one of relief: I know I can always get a job as a secretary. And that's despite the eighteen years of management and professional work that now lie between me and my last secretarial stint. These early lessons die hard.

What kept me writing all those years before I tried to sell my work, and what sent me to New York to try to get a job as a writer, were some powerful nudges from the outside, specifically from some teachers in grade school and high school. I dedicated my *Burn Marks* to them.

The first of these teachers came into my life when I was nine, and encouraged me to believe I had a gift for story-telling. The other two came when I was sixteen, the year I was going through my secretarial course. One wrote on an exam paper that my writing was a rare gift which should be nurtur-ed. That paper was for some years my talisman, until my father, in a fit of fury, burned it along with all my other child-hood and adolescent writings – stories, poems and diaries.

I'd like to be able to look back and see what I said then when I was nine and sixteen, see if I can detect in my words what those three adults found – I think if I could, it might give me more confidence in what I undertake today. But as that's not possible I continue to grope my way more or less in a fog, trying to turn the stories in my head into books.

Those three teachers couldn't overcome all the negative messages I was taking in at home. But they did give me enough of a spark that I kept writing, for myself, privately, until I came to a point in my life where I was strong enough to try to write for publication.

Despite the sad or self-pitying tone of these remarks, my life has been very lucky. In the first place I had these teachers to help me out. Not every child with a gift ever hears from anyone that word of encouragement that keeps a spark alive. But I had three people who gave me that word.

Second, I was lucky to be born when I was. I came of age when the great feminist revolution of the 1970s was begin-ning to crest. And the excitement of that movement, of the support of many women reaching out to help each other, affected me profoundly. The women's movement gave me the beginnings of a voice. It also gave me the beginning of a sense of empowerment in my own life. Not only is biology not destiny, but your own particular slanted slotting upbringing is not destiny.

I was also lucky to marry a man who loves to see women driving trucks, cleaning engine heads, writing novels, or doing any other thing that makes them feel competent, even powerful in their own lives. His support has wrapped me round like a cloak, easing me through times of despair, giving me courage to hold on to my voice.

And finally, I have the rare gift of hearing from women around the world who say my work speaks to them in important ways. When I feel at my bluest, I turn to these readers for nurture: readers and writers sustain each other in important ways. One cannot exist without the other and I feel honoured by the support I get from readers. I hope we will journey together for many years.

From a 'Meet the Author' event at the
1991 Festival

JANICE GALLOWAY

Janice Galloway was born in Ayrshire, where she taught for ten years. She now makes a living from writing and from reviewing music. Since her first publication in the *Edinburgh Review* in 1986, her short stories have appeared in a variety of literary magazines and anthologies. Her adaptation of Radclyffe Hall's *The Well of Loneliness* was performed at Edinburgh's Theatre Workshop in May 1989.

When her first book, *The Trick is to Keep Breathing*, was published in 1990, Janice Galloway was hailed as an outstanding new novelist of intelligence and maturity. In *Blood*, her collection of short stories, one of the main subjects was fear. She writes about grim urban realities with wit, clarity and enormous energy. She is currently working on a new novel, scheduled for publication in spring 1994.

Previous titles include:

The Trick is to Keep Breathing
Blood

JANICE GALLOWAY

Objective Truth and the Grinding Machine or don't let the bastards etc etc

I write because I hate being told HOW IT IS. I didn't realise that for a long while. I thought it was LIFE I hated: that the unfairnesses that were explained as JUST HOW IT IS were JUST HOW IT WAS. But HOW IT IS wasn't. It was how it is made to be, how it was presented as being by certain groups whose own best interests were being served by the presentation of their best interests as fact. As OBJECTIVE TRUTH. This, dear reader, is HOW I FOUND OUT.

When I was very wee I didn't read at all. My mother sang Elvis and Peggy Lee songs, the odd Rolling Stones hit as they appeared. They gave me a notion of how relationships between the sexes were conducted (there were NO MEN in our house), the meaning of LURV, a sprinkling of American-isms (to help conceal/sophisticate the accent I had been born into and which my mother assured me was IGNORANT and COMMON) and a basic grounding in ATTITUDE. This last (the words to Blue Suede Shoes are carved on my heart) was the MOST USEFUL one. In fact, the ONLY USEFUL one.

I was reading by the time I went to primary. I know I was

73

reading before I went to primary because I got a row for it when I did go. Reading before educationally permissible was pronounced to be VERY DETRIMENTAL TO HER IN CLASS. This was true because I had to do it again their way (*Janet and John* and *The Dog with the Red Ball*) which was BORING but a necessary part of my SOCIALISATION. This did not trouble me. Books were read round the class, i.e. TOO SLOW, and you got the belt if you peeked at the next page as a result of getting too interested. BOREDOM became an intrinsic part of EDUCATION. This did not trouble me either. They were the TEACHERS and not open to question. I was a biddable child. Most ARE.

At home, I read the *Bunty* (WEE SLAVEY was a role model), the *Beano* (BERYL was too removed from reality to be any encouragement), *Enid Blyton Fairy Tales* and *Folk Tales of Many Lands*. I liked those because they were full of other realities. Other ways of being, I suppose. When the MANY LANDS ran out, I tried to take MYTHOLOGY and WORLD RELIGION books from the adult shelves of the local library. The local librarian (Defender of Books from the inquiry of grubby people and children) smacked my hands and told me I wasn't allowed THOSE ONES: I would neither like nor understand them and was only SHOWING OFF. This was another timely lesson in the value of hiding NATURAL ENTHUSIASM because it sometimes annoyed people in authority who preferred to inculcate OBEDIENCE TO RULES as more appropriate. I ran errands to the same library for my nineteen-years-older sister who read six books a week and HIT ME if I brought back books by women authors because WOMEN CANNY WRITE. Other HITTING OFFENCES included being sent a subscription to *Reader's Digest* by an uncle, asking to watch *A Midsummer Night's Dream* on the telly and keeping a diary. ENJOYING WORDS WAS AN OCCUPATION FRAUGHT WITH PAIN.

My mother read biographies of film stars. Some of those were women but they had had the sense to get other people to write the words down for them. She also read the odd novel from a stack on top of the cupboard shelf which I could not reach. ANGELIQUE featured on the spines but I already knew enough to know she was not the AUTHOR. I also knew these were DIRTY but never found out for sure. My father had apparently been a reader between drinks but that was only hearsay.

At ten, I accidentally wrote a novel in blue biro and pencil in which the lead character, a BOY my own age who lived in a COLONISED NATION, died horribly after saving his family and village from NORMANS, whereupon the aforementioned family realise what bastards they had been to him TOO LATE. My mother found it but didn't tell my sister. She lit the fire with it.

Secondary school proved mother and sister uncannily PERCEPTIVE. Women couldny write. There were NONE, not one, not even SAFELY DEAD ones like Jane Austen or the Brontës as a class text. Women who appeared in the books by men were for the purposes of ogling or fucking, allowing male character development or SYMBOLISM. This helped reinforce the notion that women were NOT INTER-ESTING in themselves and that ART did not concern itself with them. Not them, US. This suggested that books did not need to have any connection with anything I could feel as REAL in order to be ART. In fact, the LESS REAL they felt, the more likely they were to be ART or ANY GOOD. This troubled me a little but not overmuch. I had other battles to fight. Like refusing to say SORRY to the Head of Girls after I did not turn up to collect my FREE DINNER TICKETS one week (You get these at the Taxpayer's expense and you will USE THEM DILIGENTLY with a PROPER RESPECT for that fact) and having the posh boys from Largs think I was an Easy Lay because I SPOKE COORSE and wore short plastic skirts. Besides, books let you down. I was not in love with BOOKS. I was in love with MUSIC. I was going to be a MUSICIAN because I ENJOYED IT (something somewhere knew the only ART worth a damn was ART you could FEEL) and also because it was a place where WOMEN got to shine LEGITIMATELY (ACTRESS would have done but that wasn't on offer). The first lesson taught me MOZART was pronounced MOTZART and not as spelled on the biscuit tin at home. His notes sounded even more beautiful than his name. MUSIC kept getting better and better. Between Purcell and Byrd, Britten, Warlock and Gesualdo, I read and sang

FOLK SONGS. I had always sung popular songs but these ones were OLD. And they had WOMEN IN: being pregnant and deserted, working and raising children, coping and GETTING THEIR OWN BACK OCCASIONALLY. This was not ART of course, but EXCITING. DANGEROUS even. My mind was made up. I would study MUSIC and be a CREDIT TO MYSELF. Also it would be one in the eye for Head of Girls who said I was NOT UNIVERSITY MATERIAL. The day I got accepted, I turned up at school in trousers and got sent home. This did not trouble me. I was taking the MUSIC and getting out.

I visited Hillhead, peering out the filthy windows of a 59 and knowing this was THE PLACE. This was where I could STUDY and allow my NATURAL ENTHUSIASM out to play. I would revel in GREAT WORKS OF MUSIC and ponder the meaning of PROFOUND LITERARY TEXTS. I couldn't wait.

Of my ENGLISH LITERATURE syllabus, less than two of the authors on the set list were female. My MUSIC LIST seemed not to know women – or SCOTLAND – existed at all. There were no folk songs. In my third year, I cried a lot and they let me have a year out. I was suffering from a BROKEN HEART. I went back and finished only because my TUTOR said GIRLS OFTEN GAVE UP, it was nothing to be ashamed of. I could no longer listen to MUSIC. There was only one thing for it.

TEACHING. Against all expectation, I ENJOYED IT. On teaching practice, I turned up at school in trousers and was sent home. Nonetheless, I taught ENGLISH for ten years. The store cupboard was familiar. When the new Higher syllabus came out, pupils were given lists to select possible reading matter from, there were thirteen women on a list of over sixty authors. Of those, ten, including Austen, the Brontës and Jessie Kesson were LOVE AND ROMANCE: Muriel Spark's *Prime of Miss Jean Brodie* was a SCHOOL STORY. Somebody gave me Joanna Russ's *How to Suppress Women's Writing* by mistake. It troubled me a lot. It taught me the word CANON.

With this word, all sorts of THINGS in the background of my experience came to the front. With this word, I could make CONNECTIONS. I could CONNECT reading lists with straitjackets, the university with Saltcoats Library and my sister with Hitler. Russ's book helped SOMETHING IMPORTANT to click into place, i.e. that traditional CANON, the 'recognised' body of work that is 'significant' in 'literary terms', the one they'd been firing at me through school and university, was simply a CONSTRUCT. Moreover, a very NARROW CONSTRUCT and not, as some would have us believe, OBJECTIVE TRUTH. Women not only wrote, not only wrote well, but wrote well and ABUNDANTLY if you knew where and how to LOOK. The CANON had marginalised our experience and our voice. HOW IT IS, WASN'T. It was (da capo) HOW IT WAS MADE TO BE BY CERTAIN GROUPS WHOSE OWN BEST INTERESTS WERE BEING SERVED BY THE PRESENTATION OF THEIR BEST INTERESTS AS FACT.

IT WAS LIKE FINDING THE NOSE ON MY FACE.

It was better because, for the first time since I learned how to pronounce MOZART, it suggested the chance for real GROWTH in place of RESTRICTION, FREEDOMS in places of RULES. I remembered something I seemed to have known from a long time ago. I remembered Elvis. And I knew three things. I knew:

(a) I didn't need to believe any second-hand definitions of ART or GOOD or REAL any more;

(b) I didn't have to believe a thing that didn't FEEL like it was TRUE or pretend it did FEEL REAL if it didn't;

and

(c) anything calling itself JUST HOW IT IS stunk like a month-old kipper.

My mother was dead: I had not seen my sister for years. I had nothing to lose but my chains.

I started writing.

RUMER GODDEN

Rumer Godden was born in 1907 in Sussex and moved to India with her family when she was six months old. She spent most of her childhood in East Pakistan, and at the age of twelve was sent to Britain to complete her education in a convent. She then returned to India, where she ran a dance school. She lived with her children in the Himalayan foothills of Kashmir for the duration of the Second World War, at the end of which she returned to England, still writing, and saw her novels *Fugue in Time* and *Black Narcissus* made into successful films. She now lives in Dumfriesshire near her family.

Rumer Godden's literary works are extensive and varied – nearly sixty books of fiction, autobiography, children's books, short stories and poetry. She is a storyteller in the best tradition. Favourite themes in her writing include religion, children, dance and her Pekingese dogs. She was the winner of the Whitbread Award for her children's book *The Diddakoi*.

Previous titles include:

FOR ADULTS

The River
Black Narcissus
Fugue in Time
Two under the Indian Sun
In this House of Brede

The House with Four Rooms
The Battle of the Villa Fiorita
An Episode of Sparrows
Coromandel Sea Change

FOR CHILDREN

The Diddakoi
Fu-Dog
A Kindle of Kittens

Mr McFadden's Hallowe'en
Listen to the Nightingale

RUMER GODDEN

Trusting in Providence

'Are you still writing?' people say to me – as if it were some kind of phenomenon. It is not a phenomenon at all; it is perfectly natural because you don't give up writing until writing gives you up. Suddenly the ideas and the urge disappear. It's called writer's block and thankfully it hasn't happened to me yet. Just how the ideas and the urge to write come to a novelist is one of the mysteries of our trade. Why should one thing, out of thousands of things you experience, read about, hear about, suddenly say 'write about me'? Sometimes it happens after a long time, as with my book *Coromandel Sea Change*. It is the story of one week in an old-fashioned hotel in Southern India. I went there for three weeks fifty years ago and I had forgotten it completely. Suddenly in the middle of the night (and these moments are most inconvenient) I was woken by that very hotel: I saw it, I saw the colours, I smelled the scents and I heard the sound of the sea.

Memory is one of the riches of old age. Of course it doesn't mean that you don't forget things – I couldn't tell you probably what I did yesterday. But old age brings a patina to what you hear, see and experience every day. To a young person a sunrise, however beautiful or striking, is simply a sunrise. To me it evokes other sunrises, high on Tiger Hill above Darjeeling, or a sunrise after dancing all night, coming out feet tired, heart buoyant, to go home with the first rays of the sun warming the cool air. An old person can be like the householder in the New Testament who brought out of his treasure-house things old and new.

This does not mean that I live in an enchanted world – far from it. There were years when I had it very hard, and I knew what despair, real poverty and loneliness meant. I don't regret them; they gave me more understanding and oddly enough, trust. I firmly believe in providence. When I came back to England from India after the Second World War, without a husband, with two small children and no money, everyone told me I must get a job. I was even offered a good one. But somehow I had the strength to pursue only writing. It wasn't easy. I got up at four to write and worked again when the children had gone to bed. I have never grudged hard work and in fact I work in the most taxing way possible. I write by hand and deliberately slowly, slow, because aren't books made of thought? Even a typewriter goes too fast for me.

When I was a young writer, I and my contemporaries wanted one thing more than anything else for our books. Not money or success (though of course we wanted those too!); we wanted our books to last. I suppose I have had a small share of that. *Black Narcissus*, which was written in 1938, has never been out of print in one form or another in some part of the world.

I am often dismissed as a storyteller, not a literary person, but if I could choose which of two very great writers I could be, Proust or Stevenson, I would unhesitatingly plump for Robert Louis. I was recently sent a long questionnaire by my publisher, wanting to know everything about me from the day I was born. Everything in fact that has nothing to do with writing. I am afraid that most of my answers were negative. Education – in my case almost nil. Qualifications – none except for dancing. Politics or hobbies – none. The last question, however, temporarily floored me: What makes you think that your books are different from anyone else's? At first I decided not to answer it as it seemed to me impertinent. Then I reflected and began to see that it is a vital question, relevant and one to which there is only one answer.

Because they are written by *me*. That sounds conceited *but it isn't*, because *every one* of us writers ought to be able to say it if we keep to our integrity and are not deflected by considerations of popularity – or more usually money. It doesn't mean either that we *think we are good writers*: some of us with that unmistakable hallmark have an *appalling* style – but it is our own.

And it is the only way for all of us to *fulfilment* because:

Each mortal thing does one thing and the same;
Deals out that being indoor each one dwells;
Selves – goes itself, *myself* it speaks and spells
Crying 'What I do is me, for that I came'.

'For that I came'. *Storytellers* you know you are *born not made*.

From a talk given at the 1991 Festival.

MARY WESLEY

Mary Wesley published her first novel in 1983 at the age of seventy, since when she has rapidly gained an audience for her warm, humorous and vividly paced stories. Of her newly acquired fame and fortune, she says, 'I started when most people finish, that's why I'm an oddity. I had this curious feeling for years that I was waiting to do something – to write. But the gestation took a hell of a long time.'

Previous titles include:

Jumping the Queue
Harnessing Peacocks
The Camomile Lawn
The Vacillations of
  Poppy Carew

Not That Sort of Girl
A Sensible Life
The Sixth Seal
Haphazard House
A Dubious Legacy

MARY WESLEY

Both Sides of the Pendulum

I never went properly to school. I had a nanny until I was three and then I had sixteen foreign governesses. We were read aloud to a great deal, by my mother, my grandmother and then the governesses. Although they read in French or Italian or German, my family read in English and we got through the works of Dickens, Scott and Stevenson, and so on. I must admit I was dreadfully bored a lot of the time as a child. It was a rather restricted childhood as we were forever moving and I grew up knowing no other children. I've always spent my time inventing stories for myself. I remember when I was in my early twenties driving along with a boyfriend and I said something about making up stories and he turned to me and said, 'You should have grown out of that.' I reminded him of that the other day – he's a year older than I am and he was rather cross.

I spent some time at a finishing school in Paris until my mother found we were not properly chaperoned so I left there and 'came out'. After going to a few balls my mother remembered I was only sixteen and said, 'Good God, you shouldn't be going to all these parties!' So I was taken in again and sent to a domestic science school to learn how to cook and clean the silver and wash glass, which has come in jolly useful since. I came out again and started to go out with rather clever men who kept remarking how ignorant I was.

Then I went to the London School of Economics where I became fascinated by international politics. It was a good period because the school was full of angry Yugoslavs, Hungarians and Czechs. They appealed to me quite a lot.

Living through the war was both very frightening and exhilarating. There was a sort of counterbalance of fear with an atmosphere of frivolity. People were always having parties in case they might never have one again. Men you might have been dancing with one evening were killed the next morning; you never got used to that. To start with I worked in the War Office which was very interesting. I wrote *The Camomile Lawn* as an exercise to try to get the feeling and atmosphere of the war in print.

I was very broke when my husband died and I existed on a widow's pension with a child still at school. It was hard and difficult and it's very boring being badly off because there is so little you can do. I knew I could write by then but I blocked. I wrote a children's book which I became so obsessed by that I was praying like mad for somebody at Mass one day and suddenly burst out laughing as I realised I was praying for one of the characters in the book. I started writing *Jumping the Queue*, which somehow helped me get over the trauma of my husband dying.

Sometimes I know how a book is going to end, but often I go to bed in an absolute rage of despair because I don't know what's happening next. I'm terribly secretive and don't tell anybody during the process of writing. In theory I work every day, but in practice I don't. When I'm into a book then I do keep sort of office hours and most of my friends know better than to ring me between nine and five, but I'm probably not working. I may be gardening or doing something else, but my mind is ticking over. I make notes all the time because I forget things so easily and I get ideas in bed or in the bath or when I'm cooking. I write in long-hand and can't type. Everybody asks me why I don't use a word-processor but I would not dream of it – I hate anything mechanical. When I'm finally and relatively satisfied a lovely girl types it up for me and if necessary I re-write. It's very laborious.

When I finish a book I feel every single time that I really

ought to re-write but cannot bring myself to do it. I think that this is the last idea I shall ever hold in my head, but each time I finish a book another one is sort of creeping up. It's very strange, like a dream. Sometimes some very small thing I observe will set off a whole train of thought, or a phrase I overhear somehow begins to create a character. It's a mysterious occupation, writing. But as long as that happens I may be able to go on. Sometimes I enjoy writing and enjoy the aftermath, having written it, both sides of the pendulum. If it goes well it's lovely and if you're stuck it's misery. It's a big mistake to think, 'I've had a good day' – the next day I'll read it and it's absolute rubbish.

God forbid, I'm not a message-giver: I hope I'm an entertainer. I can never let go of the maverick figure in my fiction. I suppose I could admit to being maverick myself. I have met some very wild people, and plenty of conventional people – but behind the convention there is always something else. It fascinates me. We all pretend to be so good and so conventional, whereas one may be thinking something quite different. It's one of the delights of listening to people talk – you see people being frightfully polite to each other but you know they are longing to get away from this bore and they're too polite to say. That is the veneer of civilisation. When I get tired of characters – this is the joy for writers – you can kill them off, which you can't in real life. And I can encourage the ones that I like, like the twins in *Not That Sort of Girl*, so vile and so nasty and vicious that I simply loved them and had to bring them back in another book.

Before I got published I wrote quite a clutch of books, all of which I threw away. I wrote some quite good poetry, my husband said, but I lost it. I don't believe in keeping traces – I think a writer's best friend should be the wastepaper basket. I did keep a diary for about ten years when I was young but I burnt it because I thought it gave too much of me away. I put it all in the boiler without a glance. Now there's a man called Mr Gottlieb at Boston University who has started buying my manuscripts and I terribly regret having thrown so much away because now I would be getting lovely dollars for them!

From an event chaired by Angela Lambert at the 1991 Festival.

The Writing Day

DEADLINES RULE OK?

EDITORS PADLOCK

LOCKED UP TILL EDIN. BOOK FESTIVAL

and not even Wild Horses are allowed to drag me away...

Illustration by Mairi Hedderwick

HUNTER DAVIES

Hunter Davies was born in Renfew in 1936, brought up in Carlisle, educated at Durham University, and now lives half the year in London and half in Loweswater. He is the author of over thirty books, including biographies of Wordsworth, Columbus, The Beatles, Beatrix Potter and George Stephenson. He has also written books for young children and teenagers, and novels for adults – the most recent being *Striker*, which was published in 1992. At present he is working on a travel biography of Robert Louis Stevenson, due out in 1994. He runs a little publishing company called Forster Davies, so little that he only publishes books written by himself, including *The Good Guide to the Lakes*. As a journalist, he worked on the *Sunday Times* where he was chief feature writer and then editor of the magazine. He wrote regular columns in *Punch* and currently writes for the *Independent*. For three years, he presented *Bookshelf* on BBC Radio 4. He has been a member of the Board of Directors of the Edinburgh Book Festival since 1990. He is married to the biographer and novelist Margaret Forster.

Previous titles include:

Here We Go Round
 the Mulberry Bush
The Beatles
William Wordsworth
In Search of
 Christopher Colombus

A Walk Around the Lakes
Striker
the *Flossie Teacake* series
the *Snotty Bumstead* series
The Glory Game

HUNTER DAVIES

Our Writing Life

Two writers in the same house: how do you manage, how do you get on, how do you share, is there any rivalry, are there any arguments, is there anyone to answer the door when the Jehovah's Witness calls.

I am often asked these questions, as I move around the planet, usually preceded by 'oh no, it was actually your wife I wanted to meet'. In most situations which slowly emerge, you can't remember how they began. Our writing life, each working from home, seems perfectly normal and ordinary to me from where I sit in my room, thinking bloody hell, why doesn't she answer that soddin door, it's her rotten turn.

We are totally different writers, different human beings with different temperaments, producing totally different sorts of stuff. That helps. And we've done it now for almost thirty years. So, patterns have formed, routines established themselves.

Margaret was the first to get a book accepted, back in 1964, with a novel about Oxford which she denies she ever wrote. I'd been struggling with plays, goodness knows why, nobody asked me, nobody said, 'give us a play, Hunt'. Actually they did, in a way, now I think back. I wrote one play based on something that happened to a friend, sent it off, and low and uphold, it was accepted by a West End director straight away who paid me a hundred pounds for a year's option. This is the boys, I thought, this is where my future lies, so I knocked out another play. This was turned down. Then the first one collapsed when the backers withdrew. I was therefore feeling pretty choked – till suddenly Margaret got a novel accepted by Jonathan Cape. (She had written an earlier one, never published.)

I thought to myself, I know her, she lives in our house – if she can do it, if she get can get a novel accepted, I'll have a go. What had bugged me up to then about trying a novel was the worry of having a plot. Then I read *Catcher in the Rye*, saw that a plot was not necessary, and did a story about a boy in a northern council house trying to get off with a girl from a semi. Like all beginners, we had no contacts, and just sent things off into the blue, getting agents' names from books or the library. Richard Simon, a young chappie at Curtis Brown, said he liked it, but felt it fell away after halfway. I worked on it, and it was taken by Heinemann and then made into a film. Ah, the 1960s. Margaret's second novel, *Georgy Girl*, also became a film. We thought that's what happened to all novels.

Margaret had been teaching, till her first novel was accepted. She gave up her day job from then on, unless you count having three children and running a house. I had been working as a journalist on the *Sunday Times*, but I didn't give that up for another ten years, mainly because I enjoyed it so much. I could have done, and lived totally on books, as apart from those two films, I did The Beatles biog around the same time. It meant I was always prepared to leave the *ST*, if they asked me to do anything boring or stupid.

Margaret has stuck to her last, well two lasts, as she has become a biographer and a novelist, but I'm all over the place, doing this and that, having a go at all sorts of books. What happens in publishing, as you well know, is that when you do one sort of book that sells well, those brilliant chaps in their publishing machines say heh, can you do us another, on the same lines. After The Beatles, I got endless offers to do other pop stars. After *The Glory Game*, which was about football, I got offers to do other football books. I always refused, partly because I didn't need their money. The common denominator in my writing life has been ignorance.

I fall in love with a new subject – like Hadrian's Wall, or Wordsworth, or Columbus, or stamps – and I think now, who can I talk into a book so that I can spend a year enjoying myself.

At any one time, I can have three books on the go, which Margaret thinks is dopey. As I write, I am in the final stages of the latest *Good Guide to the Lakes*, a children's book about a little boy called Snotty, and I've just returned from Samoa, researching a biography of Robert Louis Stevenson for 1994. Right, that's enough plugs. My day is therefore fairly chaotic, trying to balance the different books at their different stages, plus doing odd broadcasts and some journalism – at the moment a weekly interview for the *Independent* which I send in by stage-coach and never go to the office. Margaret is desperate for me to keep this going. She loves having me out of the house at least once a week.

She gets up first, around 7.30, very quietly, so as not to awaken the master, goes downstairs, opens up, brings me tea and the *Independent*, pulls the curtains and switches on Radio 4. I do find my arms awfie tired in the mornings. She then exits, closing the door firmly behind her. In the old days, this was to keep out any marauding kids. Now they've left home.

I loll for about an hour, eventually getting up around nine. Now, this next bit is rather disgusting, and may offend sensitive souls. I have a bath in her left-over bath-water. Well, it saves money, saves me running my own. After my muesli, I walk round Hampstead Heath for half an hour. The bit I like best is crossing Highgate Road and seeing all the cars, bumper to bumper. I think, poor souls, there they are, dying in their cars.

I then have a cappuccino, read the post and, with a great effort, drag myself to my office about ten o'clock. We each have our own office, on different floors. I walk around mine, count the aspirins, check my collections, stare out of the window, and eventually get started, huffing and puffing, moaning and groaning.

I do like work. I adore a blank page. It's my favourite sight. Naked, virginal paper, just waiting for me to empty myself. I have no trouble filling the pages, the more the better. What I hate is re-writing, going back, trying to make things better. That's probably the real reason I do so many different things. I can't bear what I've just done, ever desperate to move on. I tell myself that even if I did rewrite, polish and hone, it would not be much better, and anyway, it would spoil the fun. That's all I'm in it for. If a day goes by and I haven't written at least five new pages, and I normally hope for ten, then I feel empty, distraught, a failure. I don't deserve a drink or a good meal till I've done my self-appointed whack, pushed on, justified my existence. It could be a disease.

All the same, I am dying for any interruptions. I jump to the phone before it rings, ever eager for some chat, some news. I listen for the second post and yes, it is me who goes down and argues the toss about Jehovah. I'm always losing things, books and notes, so I go round shouting at myself. Naturally, I need lots of breaks, from all this shouting, so I go downstairs, on the hour, to make myself some coffee. After that I go to the lavatory, on the half-hour.

Meanwhile, Her Majesty has gone to her little room at nine o'clock – *and has not moved*. She is a miracle. No, really. She sits at her little desk, from nine till one every day, and that's it. She takes no coffee, needs no lavatory, answers no phones, is out to all callers, is not interested in the post and should I be stupid enough to poke my head round her door and say er, I can't find the aspirins, I get screamed at.

My office *is* an office, filled with modern machinery, though not all working at the same time, hence the screams as I lose pages. I have an Amstrad PCW 9512 to which I've now added a Canon bubble jet printer. I have a fax machine. I have a Canon copier. And I have all this lot double because we now divide our life between London and Loweswater, spending six months in each place, with an office in each house.

Margaret, bless her, survives on one fountain pen. Remember them? Very portable, so no need for two. Plus paper, of course. I don't let her write on the desk as it does damage the surface.

At one o'clock exactly she stops, on the dot, and that's it for her creative day. When she's on a novel, she never breathes a word of it, never thinks about it, changes the subject if asked, till next day at nine when she sits down again. On a biography, her hours are the same, but this time we can't stop her talking. Every conversation gets dragged round to Daphne, or whoever. What Daphne had for her meals, what Daphne liked and didn't like.

We have a light snack made by her, a sandwich, perhaps an omelette, perhaps sardines on toast, no wine – well, okay, just a glass for me, as I have had a hard morning. Then we go out on Hampstead Heath for an enormous walk, two hours, talking the while, all the way round. Gawd knows what about. Books, sometimes. I usually leave her on the Hampstead side, then go for a cappuccino in one of four caffs to which I give my valued custom. I buy a second paper, which I sit on my own and read. I love that bit of the day. I often stand up afterwards and think now, where am I, where am I going. But don't we all.

Back home, around four, I go to my office for another two hours. Margaret, meanwhile, having finished her day's load, is on the couch downstairs, deep into a novel. She reads a new one every day, all round the year. What a hedonist. I don't think I've read a novel for pleasure since, oh dunno, Dickens was a lad.

I usually work in the evening as well, especially if I've got a panic on to finish something. I take commissions. Margaret never does. I don't watch TV, apart from football. Roughly speaking then, I work from ten to ten every day, with two hour breaks, seven days a week. Weekends are all the same to us. On the other hand, I have always taken thirteen weeks' holiday a year.

We are not in competition, in any sense, as we produce such different work. She is of course a literary person, what what, while I'm a – well, what am I – word-shifter, general hack, jack of all trades? It is nice being in the same line of work, able to discuss and understand exactly what the other is doing and feeling. We know the people in each other's life and we can rubbish the same publishers, agents and critics.

Best of all, it's like having two lives, two bites of the same cherry. It doubles all possibilities. I get as much pleasure out of her little bits of news and success as my own – another foreign right sold, an interesting magazine offer, a good review. With two of us bashing away, the post most days brings something of interest, something to cheer one of us, which is nice if you are the one plodding away on a hard bit and nothing much seems to be happening.

I have gained a lot by having a writing wife. In my early days of working from home I found it very hard to write one page, even one paragraph, sometimes one sentence, without having an audience. It was the fault of my journalistic training. In a newspaper office, you get a response after every hour or so when you hand in your piece, even if all the news editor says is 'load of rubbish, do it again, son'. With luck, you see it in print next day. Taking a year on your own to do a book is tough, when you're not very strong-willed and no one seems interested.

Er, what do you think of this page, my petal, I used to say, knocking on her door. 'Get out,' she'd say, 'I'm busy.' Oh come on, help me. 'Okay then, do a whole chapter, then I might read it.' And so she did, which was kind. Then it was two chapters, then three. In the end, thanks to her training, her discipline, her fine example, I was able to finish a whole book, with no one having read it. Now, it's often published, and she's still not read a word. Especially if it's about football, or stamps. Or what I do at home, during my working day . . .

DEBORAH MOGGACH

Deborah Moggach was born into a world of books – one of four daughters, her father is historian Richard Hough, author of some ninety books; her mother, Charlotte Hough, is an illustrator and author of numerous children's books. She lives in Camden Town, London, with her two teenage children. She has written ten novels, and adapted many of them as television series or films. She has also written a book of short stories and a stage play, *Double Take*, and recently adapted Anne Fine's *Goggle-Eyes* for BBC Television.

Deborah Moggach's tenth novel, *The Ex-Wives*, was published in 1993 and she is now adapting it for television. *The Stand-In* is being made into a Hollywood film.

WRITERS WRITING

Previous titles include:

Hot Water Man · *Stolen*

Porky

A Quiet Drink

Close to Home

The Stand-In

To Have and to Hold

You Must Be Sisters

Smile

The Ex-Wives

Driving in the Dark

DEBORAH MOGGACH

One of those 'Life in the Day' Things

Once the children have trailed off to school I'm all alone. I finish off their toast crusts and delay starting work by reading the papers from cover to cover. Apart from the posh ones I also get the *Daily Mail*; my mother lives opposite and pushes it through the letter-box like pornography. This delays things another half-hour. I read everything, right down to the mail-order ads for velour tracksuits.

With any luck, it's already ten o'clock by the time I go upstairs to work. I ignore the mess *en route*. My house is a pit, but if I cleaned it up I'd never get anything done. Paperwork lies on the stairs for months, a sort of escalating in-tray; sometimes, when the phone rings and I rush down to get it, I sort of ski down on my old bank statements. I need a wife to take care of things.

Being a writer is cheap on clothes because I can wear the same thing, day in day out. It's usually ancient trousers and airline socks. I can also economise on make-up by not washing my face. For what remains of the morning I work.

I lie on my bed, writing in long-hand with a nice new Pentel. Soon the page becomes cobwebbed with insertions and looping arrows as characters thicken up and start speaking. Before I begin a novel I have mapped it out roughly, writing pages of notes on each character and threading together the plot. This might take weeks or months. I have to know the end, otherwise I simply can't write at all – where does one begin, if one doesn't know the outcome? How does one know what to omit and what to highlight? On their journey, however, the characters might take the plot with them and gallop off, like frisky horses pulling a carriage. If it's going well, that's what they *should* do. But I must have a firm hand on the reins and finally steer them to our shared destination. I must be in charge.

Meanwhile, I doodle drawings of vulgar women down the sides of the paper. For some reason, they are usually naked or décolleté; if I'm on a train, people start craning to look. The worse my work is going the more of them appear, like uninvited guests at a party. But if I'm writing TV scripts I draw people on purpose and give them dialogue. Sometimes I just speak into the mirror, mumbling and gesticulating and laughing at my own jokes. It's a strange, solitary life, making people up and getting them to talk to you.

The morning is punctuated by mugs of Nescafé, glasses of wine and roll-ups. Also by a variety of noises-off. At the back of the house there is a railway line with a twenty-four-hour taxi garage beneath. From it comes merry reggae music and a tattoo of panel-beating. Sometimes this stops for a whole five minutes and I think everything's going to be all right. The man next door chain-smokes and coughs all day like Camille, and on the other side there's a little dog which is locked out all day. Sometimes its yaps drown out even the panel-beating. On the far side there is a day centre for people with learning difficulties. They all seem to be learning the electric guitar, and it's usually *Hey Jude*. They practise it all day until they get it almost right. Out in the street, the car alarms join in.

Meanwhile, I'm trying to work. When I've finished in long-hand I type it on to my computer. It's a hugely complicated machine – they all are, I suppose – but I've only learnt about three basic things. I've never opened its vast manuals or the volumes that go with its laser printer because once I get started on that I'd never get any work done. Besides, it's too alarming. I haven't got that sort of brain. With machines it's easy to get sidetracked. For instance, when I'm calling up a file I often get my son's homework by mistake, and spend half the morning reading 'The Pros and Cons of Bismarck's Foreign Policy'.

For lunch I eat the remains of last night's supper, maybe cold tortellinis straight from the saucepan. Sometimes I stand at the fridge dipping my finger into a tub of hummus. When I was writing a novel set in Pakistan I used to eat Marks and Spencer's pea and potato curry to get into the mood.

In the afternoon my concentration, or what there was of it, finally evaporates. I envy writers who can work all day. The most I can do, p.m., is gaze at my VAT receipts on the stairs and tell myself I'm going to get round to sorting them out. Sometimes, if I feel achieving, I wade through the litter outside and go swimming in Kentish Town Baths, or I wander around the streets looking into people's windows. This is such a trendy area that nobody has net curtains, thank goodness. In the shops I listen to people talking; what I overhear has a peculiar sharpness and vibrancy, as if I've been out of the country for months.

If a book is going well I feel weightless; it's as if I've been emptied of myself. I wander around like a ghost, seeing everything through the eyes of my fictional characters. What are their sensations, as they stand in the queue at the post office or buy a piece of smoked haddock? If some friend in the street calls out my name it gives me a jolt; it takes a moment to rejoin my real self. I've just finished a novel about a boozy old actor who lives in a flat in Maida Vale – one of those dusty old mansion blocks. When I was writing it I used to drive there and sit outside, imagining him walking in and out, taking his empties to the bottle bank and dragging his little dog behind him. I'm now going to adapt it as a TV series and so he is going to have a whole new lease of life. When I drive past now I see him standing behind his net curtains, waiting, like a waxwork, for me to activate him again.

At 4.30 my adolescent children come home from school, munching crisps and falling on my wallet like vultures. After they have cleaned me out (forty pounds for football boots, twenty pounds for an acre of rainforest) one of us has to go out to the Natwest cash dispenser to get enough money for supper. The notes come out mysteriously warm, as if someone is baking in there. Why? It's the sort of question one can think about the whole of the following morning.

My children and I have given up conversations at meals – what a relief – so in the evening we sit squashed in a row on the sofa, eating, and watching videos. We have exhausted the local shops – they've only got Kung Fu left and even *we* can't face those – and now we roam further afield for our fix. If I ever get into *Who's Who* I can list all my clubs – the Palace Video Club, the Ritz Video Club. The best thing about writing screenplays is that I don't feel guilty about watching TV; I can pretend it's work. And it's almost impossible to read someone else's novels when you're in the middle of writing one yourself. While we watch, the hamster travels over the floor in its perspex exercise ball. When the TV is really interesting we don't hear it go thump, thump down the stairs.

At night I fall asleep, gently vibrating as the freight trains travel past. Really heavy ones go by at night; it's the North London Line and I think they are the trains which carry the nuclear waste. They make the fillings in my teeth rattle. I have vivid and engrossing dreams – each night it's like entering a cinema for which I have paid no entrance fee; each night is full of surprises. I lie there in my shaking bed; sometimes, if work is going really well, I dream about the people in my books.

Writing Equipment

Illustration by Ann Ross Paterson

CANDIA McWILLIAM

Candia McWilliam was born in 1955 in Edinburgh. She was educated there and in England. After leaving Girton College, Cambridge, with a first-class honours degree, she worked for *Vogue* magazine and later as an advertising copywriter. Her first novel, *A Case of Knives*, was the joint winner of the Betty Trask Award in 1988; it was followed by *A Little Stranger* in 1989. She lives with her husband in Oxford, where she is at work on her third book, a novel about the sea. She has three children.

Previous titles include:

A Case of Knives
A Little Stranger

CANDIA McWILLIAM

The Charm of the Verithin

I started writing because I was big and fat. If ballet or skating or some other challenge to gravity had been possible, I might have dreamed of taking it up. The girls' games in our Edinburgh street were skipping, hopscotch or Mums and Dads which was mostly pram-pushing (a doll or a furious, bonneted cat under the covers). I was any good only at the last, but it was common knowledge that I couldn't do the pram-pushing, because my height had me in demand as a Dad, and that meant you have to go off to work and leave the mothers and children to their business.

Work, I knew from observing my own father, was pencils and paper. Having acquired a second-hand naval ledger with marbled boards, already half-filled with inked charts and logs, I set to filling it, while the child-sized children carried on with real life around me. In summer I sat on the granite doorstep. Occasionally a neighbour would tell my mother that I was bound to get a chill on my kidneys like that. It was pleasantly cold, adding the touch of rigour that I liked because it made me feel like a risk-taker. In winter I sat at my mother's kitchen table at which she cooked and painted and drew. Both of us enjoyed experimenting with writing equipment. She was fond of Indian ink and a cochineal-pink tinct that came in a circular bottle with a soft rubber dropper. Our most gimmicky find was a twelve-colour ball-pen, a thick transparent tube down which the differently-coloured biro-stalks would flex, clicking into place with a snappy ratchet. Some of the colours smelt quite distinct, so that a blue doodle or a line of red writing had its own aroma. The yellow had a tough banana sweetness like that of foods intended to taste of the real thing, a kind of hyper-banana. Its equivalent in the context of strawberries has all but killed off the power of the real strawberry smell to recall lost summers.

We tried out less orthodox tools, once filling an icing bag with a mixture of Lepage's runny gum and silver glitter-dust. Our slipping twinkly words eventually dried and set like sparkly toffee. You could snap them off and pulverise them. The paper we used was sugar paper from the tobacconist, MacDonalds, at Canonmills. My mother had a hoard of good paper she had left over from art school, but she saved it up, and it is still unused, although she has been dead for twenty-nine years.

From time to time, I had the treat of a visit to number 5 Charlotte Square, the headquarters of The National Trust for Scotland; a secretary there was kind and typed at astounding speed for me cats made of capital letters. She let me take home samples of copy paper, grey, peach and the minty green and toothpaste pink that are tonal cousins. White I prized most, with its close grain like the inside of a forearm.

The least durable writing instrument my mother provided was several trays of inedible burnt biscuits and five ample ampoules of barbarically coloured icing – parrot-green, monoxide-pink and so on – each ready to deploy once its teat was snipped. A squeeze to the tacky bladder, and we were away. It was quite good for spelling adjustment, since you could remove any inappropriately lettered biscuit. Then, as now, the words I had trouble with were across, privilege and judgment.

Certainly the most thrilling drawing or writing implement was my father's Flomaster pen, a simple but unwieldy capsule of steel with a dense wick bringing the highly alcoholic black ink to the tip. It would now have the heavy chic of a contraption like the Zippo cigarette-lighter. To watch my father with this Flomaster was to be, among its fumes, a passive solvent-abuser. Before achieving the graceful line it eventually produced, the Flomaster had to be wooed, warmed, shaken, splattered, soothed. While he drew, my father held his untipped cigarette in his teeth as though it was his last gasp at air, and concentrated so hard that each breath rattled loud in the silence. The Flomaster's most memorable achievements seemed to me to be the creatures with which our basement came to be populated – seven-foot-high peculiar beasts, reminiscent of nineteenth-century zoological illustrations in their combination of literalness and fantasy. My favourite was the lyre bird, next to a hatching egg, from which was emerging slowly its quivering offspring, a tuning fork. The tribe of these creatures increased during any prolonged hostility between my parents.

The strongest stationery fixation I nurtured around this time, between the ages of about four and six, was with Crayola crayons, stubby natty tubes of wax in matching paper wrappers that unwrapped to reveal as much crayon as you needed at the twist of a – no doubt patented – embedded length of button-twine.

One profligate Christmas morning, I found that I had been left overnight twenty-four Crayolas, in their smart pack with its lozenge of window. There was new snow outside my room's own window. My crayons were waxy-cool. To see and feel them at their best, I zipped the button-twine up to the top on the wrapper of every one of the twenty-four, exploding my gift of colours in one go.

Eagle Verithin crayons came next, costing one shilling and eightpence. My parents didn't use the crayons most children had for school, Lakeland Derwent colours, for their work. They had two declared reasons for this: the Lakeland's tendency to sharp snags in the pigment and the fragility of the coloured core if you dropped a crayon by mistake. They were certain that the colour of a Lakeland went back to chalk if it were dropped. Next to leaving a paintbrush in water, dropping a crayon was the most frowned-upon thing I could do. The charm of the Verithins for me was their sharpenability – they came to a point like an arrow – and the names they bore on their flanks. Because of this charm and the hours I spent sharpening pencils to nothing but long coils of wooden peel and an inch of point, I was not to use my parents' Eagle Verithins. To me the name was as thrilling as Hispano Suiza or Aston Martin. By the time I was eight, I had a fleet of Flesh, Magenta, Rose Pink and Sea Green Verithins, purchased from a sparkling crayon bar at Aitken Dott in Hanover Street. I propped up that bar Saturday after Saturday, slipping off now and then to covet the Faber-Castell pastels in their cedar box with the laterally hooking golden clasp.

Black and white got me in the end, though. My godfather was a calligrapher and each birthday brought from him a new treatise on lettering, set of exercise-sheets or reservoir pen. The thank-you letters for these cannot have reassured him, set roundly in the Marion Richardson hand taught Edinburgh girls at the time. Some years before adolescence brings its preoccupation with appearance, however, girls decide to make themselves interesting by developing some new tic to their writing, reflexed pot-hooks, or tied-up f's. As one might go blonde, I went italic overnight, and write a bastard italic still.

Only-children have a taste for solitude that can be a help for a writer, though I have seen writers at work with children yammering around them, and saw it often in my own childhood. Perhaps for such writers the rush and fuss add to a nourishing context, perhaps they do not impinge on one capable of total absorption. Having populated my only-childhood with the invented characters whose doings filled the second-hand seaman's ledger, I failed to pick up many other aptitudes or skills. I just acquired more paper and continued, dreaming as fat children do of being weightless, of flying swift and invisible over and among events. Writing is the closest approach to it I have found.

DOUGLAS DUNN

(Photo: Fay Godwin)

Douglas Dunn was born in 1942 and brought up in Inchinnan in Renfrewshire. His collections of poetry have won several literary prizes including the Somerset Maugham Award, the Hawthornden Prize and a Cholmondley Award. *Elegies* won the Whitbread Book of the Year Award for 1985. He was a freelance writer for over twenty years and is now Professor in the School of English at the University of St Andrews, where he is also Director of the St Andrews Scottish Studies Institute. He is a member of the Scottish Arts Council and its Literature Committee. Douglas Dunn lives in Tayport in north Fife.

Previous titles include:

Elegies
Secret Villages (short stories)
Selected Poems 1965-1983
Northlight
Scotland – An Anthology

The Faber Book of Twentieth-
  Century Scottish Poetry
Dante's Drum-kit
  (November 1993)

DOUGLAS DUNN

The Pencil: A History

(A review of Henry Petroski's book of the same title, published by Faber & Faber)

As something to write with a pencil is cute engineering.
For how did they manage to squeeze that cylindrical lead
Into the timber to make what we all find endearing
Even when marking exams in satirical red?

Professor Petroski knows more about pencils than anyone –
Discovery's digits, the fingers in tune with the mind,
Engineers sketching and dreaming of what can be done,
Transferring from paper to substance and something designed.

Far back in the Freudian distance the Latin word *penis*
Crops up in its origin, meaning 'a tiny wee tail' –
Royal Sovereign, Conté and Derwent, Faber and *Venus*:
Those monarchs of pencils are not quite exclusively male.

In Primary 1 they first taught us to write on a slate.
Diminutive Romans, we formed every letter by squeak;
Then that Day of the Pencils came round – worth the wait,
Though you sharpened them down to a stub in less than a
    week.

Pencil-box Kids, each with selections of colours and Hs and
    Bs;
Sweet-smelling shavings, the point that was sharp as a dart;

115

A 2B for tickling the back of a neck – and how she said
'Please!'
Desk-top graffiti, the sums and the juvenile art.

Computerised reason and drafting are all very well
But you can't pick your nose with a screen, and keyboards
won't do
When it comes to that cedary, graphite-and-alphabet smell,
While hardware and gadgetry leave you with nothing to
chew.

Ball-points and fibretips search for invented perfection
But pencils are precious as paper is. Alloy and wood –
A pencil's a symbol of making; earth grants its affection
When what man gets up to with nature is useful and good.

Petroski puts pressure on more than the point of his pencil.
'Two cultures' are One in his book. Controversy dies:
Artists and scientists using that common utensil
Dream up what they do and it's all in the same enterprise.

So read it and find out that life's a perpetual quest
For what can be decently made, and then be improved.
With stories and pictures he shows you how pencils
progressed
From a stick in the sand to the mass-produced pencils you've
loved.

ROSAMUNDE PILCHER

Born in Cornwall in 1924, Rosamunde Pilcher was encouraged to put pen to paper from an early age. Her father was working in Burma and her Scottish mother was left to bring up two daughters virtually single-handed. At the outbreak of the Second World War, she left school to start work with the Foreign Office. A year later, she joined the WRNS and served in Portsmouth and Trincomalee, Sri Lanka with the East Indies fleet. It was during this time in Sri Lanka that she began writing seriously and by the time she was eighteen, her first story had been bought by *Woman & Home*. Since that time, Rosamunde Pilcher has sold more stories to *Good Housekeeping* in America than any other author.

At the end of the war, she married Graham Pilcher, who was still recovering from wounds suffered at the crossing of the Rhine with the Highland Division. They left Cornwall and moved to Dundee where they still live today. They have four grown-up children and eight grandchildren.

Previous titles include:

The Shell-Seekers
The End of Summer
Wild Mountain Thyme
September
The Day of the Storm

The Empty House
Another View
The Carousel
Flowers in the Rain

ROSAMUNDE PILCHER

The Smell of Blue Quink

When I was a child, there was this writer, Dorothy Black, who contributed to a profusion of women's magazines, and later found fame in the United States. Dorothy Black was married to a young army officer, serving abroad, and because managing on his skimpy pay was an uphill task, she augmented the family bank balance by writing short stories set in the exotic backgrounds in which she found herself.

My mother, one of British India's grass-widows, knew this lady. As did her friend, Mrs Pennell. One afternoon Mrs Pennell came to tea, and they talked of Dorothy Black, marvelling at her enterprise and acumen, and letting slip that she probably earned about a thousand pounds a year.

This was in the early 1930s. I, listening avidly, was deeply impressed. A thousand pounds a year was riches indeed. The idea took hold and clung. I liked reading books and writing my own stories. Surely, it would be the perfect career, because one could be a married lady and have babies at the same time, and never have to go to a horrible office to earn money, nor – dreaded prospect – do a course of Domestic Science and end up cooking institutional meals for some school or other.

Thus, at an early age, my mind was made up. Writing was to be my vocation. So, everything that happened, that I witnessed, that I read, that I watched in the cinema, was streamed into my over-active imagination, and stored away for possible future use.

As well, I was bewitched by the mechanisms of writing. By sharp pencils, new exercise books, the smell of blue Quink. Notebooks were my passion. Once on a long car journey my father gave me a notebook and a new pencil and told me to keep a diary. But before we had gone three miles, I was already busily occupied in the back seat, writing a play.

Another time, I asked for a loose-leaf book for Christmas, but when I got it, it was so beautiful that not a word was written in it for three months. The empty pages, pure and unsullied, contained so much promise that I couldn't bear to risk failure and destroy their potential. Eventually, I wrote a poem about a man escaping from a dungeon. It was not a very worthy effort.

The war, starting when I was fourteen, put an end to the only way of life I had ever known. Suddenly, everything was lightless, blacked-out, anxious, difficult and boring. My father went back into the Royal Navy, and the family, willy-nilly, followed, to coal-crusted Cardiff and a horrible flat that boiled in summer and froze in winter.

But, because of the War, one really good thing happened. My mother's sister, who had emigrated, was married and settled in Philadelphia. Patriotically Anglophile, she pondered ways to make our lives brighter. Food parcels were one possibility, or even clothes, but sensibly enough, she decided that what we really needed was a little cheer, and sent us, every month, for the whole war, the *Ladies Home Journal*.

It was, in those days, an excellent magazine, a sister-paper to the *Saturday Evening Post*, and its packed and shiny pages held treats on every page.

Growing up as I was in austere wartime Britain, the lavish advertisements for food, clothes, cars, cosmetics, scents, toys, and every sort of luxury, were my first experience of glorious consumerism.

The reading matter was even better. Articles covered a range of subjects, and provided an insight into a totally foreign way of life. (And yet the Americans were our cousins!) But the fiction was the best.

The Americans, since Mark Twain and O. Henry, had

always been the master of the short story, and the short stories I read in the *Ladies Home Journal* had a crispness, a shape, and an edge to them, that could not be compared to the hopelessly romantic, or homely and predictable tales offered up by *Woman's Weekly* or *My Home*. At an impressionable age, this whole new concept of women's fiction was like a revelation, and the steady diet of American professionalism probably taught me more about my craft than any School of Journalism could ever have achieved.

As well as four or five short stories, the paper also ran two serials in every issue. These were new novels, already bought by eminent publishing houses, and were presented uncut, and in their full entirety. As well, they were accompanied by the most brilliant illustrations. You only had to see the picture, double spread in living colour, across the glossy pages, to know that you simply had to read the book, and follow the story through for the five months of its run. In the *Ladies Home Journal*, I discovered Daphne du Maurier, Elizabeth Goudge and Nancy Mitford, as well as some of the most accomplished American writers of that time. This was no junk reading. This was for real.

Writing and reading ran together. As I read, I wrote for myself. As I learned, I practised and gained experience. At sixteen I took my courage into both hands, and submitted a first story (painfully typed on my father's typewriter) to Miss Winifred Johnson, who worked for the Camrose stable, and edited three magazines a month, two monthlies and a weekly. She sent the story back, but with a charming letter, realising, perhaps, how young I was.

I hadn't quite got the hang of it yet, she told me, but soon, I would. Everything I wrote, I must send to her.

Professional encouragement at the start of any career is a gift without price. All through my last months at school, through secretarial college, and a short and unrewarding stint at the Foreign Office, I was writing. The typescripts piled up. Then I joined the Women's Royal Naval Service and eventually was sent overseas, to Trincomalee in Sri Lanka.

I worked on a submarine depot ship, crossing the blue waters of the harbour in a spanking white pinnace, crewed by sun-bronzed seamen. A good way to go to work. In more ways than one. One afternoon, sweaty and inkstained after a day labouring in the unbearbable heat of the Confidential Book Office, I decided that it was time I went back to my other job. My real work. Returning to Quarters in the Officers' Liberty Boat, a short story neatly resolved itself into my head, with two main characters, and a beginning, a middle and an end.

Back in Quarters, unshowered and still wearing my filthy white uniform, I sat on my bunk, with a portable typewriter, nicked from the girl who slept in the next bed, and wrote. Beneath the rattling keys, the story told itself, without interruption or hesitation. At the bottom of the last page I typed, triumphantly, THE END.

I stuffed the pages into an envelope and sent the package back to England and my father, with instructions to him to type a fair copy and submit it to Miss Johnson.

He did not let me down. Two weeks later, a young seaman from the Signals Office delivered the telegram into my hands: JOHNSON BOUGHT STORY FIFTEEN GUINEAS. CONGRATULATIONS. DAD.

An ecstasy of accomplishment. I had done it. I could do it again. I was on my way.

Writing For
Children

Illustration by Shirley Hughes

SHIRLEY HUGHES

Shirley Hughes, illustrator of more than two hundred children's books, was born in West Kirby, near Liverpool. She studied drawing and costume design at Liverpool School of Art, and drawing at the Ruskin School of Drawing, Oxford. Since then, she has worked continuously as a freelance illustrator, both of her own and other authors' texts. She is best known for her warm, affectionate drawings of chubby children in her own books. Her many awards include the Kate Greenaway Medal for *Dogger*, and the prestigious Eleanor Farjeon Award for her services to children's literature.

She now lives in North Kensington with her ex-architect husband. Her own three children are grown-up, but she regularly spends time drawing and talking to children in libraries, schools and playgroups.

Previous titles include:

Bathwater's Hot
Noisy
Colours
Out and About
Angel Mae
Wheels
The Snow Lady
Giving

Bouncing
The *Alfie* books
Up and Up
Chips and Jessie
Dogger
Moving Molly
Stories by Firelight

SHIRLEY HUGHES

A Life Drawing

I find it highly gratifying to be included among writers. I regard myself as primarily an illustrator, with writing coming very much second. I don't think I could cope with the pressure of sitting down in front of a typewriter or word processor and dredging up from within myself ideas, plots and characters which are expressed only in words. It's too tough and draining a prospect. Which is why I admire people who do it so much. I couldn't get going without the pleasantly tactile preliminaries of assembling pens and brushes and squeezing out tubes of gouache paint.

I live a settled kind of life, having inhabited the same house and been married (happily) to the same man for nearly forty years. But every day in the workroom I plunge into a world of high romance, risk and adventure. An added bonus is that once things have reached a certain stage you can also listen to music – jazz, in my case (it can't be *too* demanding) and of course dear old Radio 4.

Doing your own picture book is rather like making a film. The words are unthinkable without the imagery. The pictures are not added later to make the thing look more attractive, they are an integral part of the narrative. The ideas float about for a long time like icebergs, mostly submerged. Mine are images in my head of somebody (usually a child) doing something. Alfie, for instance, a four-year-old hero of mine already at grips with the complexities of life, first surfaced running up the street ahead of his mum, who came trundling behind with the shopping and the baby in the buggy. He was eager to get in first and, it seemed to me, urgently required to get into the story. I had no thought at this point that there would be more than one book about him. And I had certainly no idea that his baby sister, Annie Rose, would emerge as such a strong and single-minded character in her own right.

The text is a matter of writing around the pictures in my head and, some time later, as part of the pattern of the page. I reach for a pencil at a very early stage to get down some roughs. I need to know what the characters look like. This process helps to crystallise the plot.

With picture book texts, the fewer words the better. But that isn't to say that they are all that easy to write. The greatest danger is of over-writing (as many skilled writers of older fiction tend to do). The aim is to hone it down and down, and to make it flow rhythmically, like a phrase of music, in and out of the pictures. It should end up sweetly and satisfyingly within the thirty-two-page (or twenty-four-page) format, including prelims and endpapers, which is usually all that the strictures of colour printing will allow. Most importantly it should be bearable for grown-ups and older siblings to read not once, but over and over again.

For this very young age group the background of the story, much of the characterisation and humour, is there to be discovered in the pictures. Accent is on the word 'discovered' because you are trying to stimulate that delightful kind of dialogue which develops when a small child is being read to. He or she is commenting on and contributing to the story, and the close observation of every detail in the picture is all part of the pleasure. It's a first introduction to fiction which is not to be missed. I don't think I am consciously thinking about all this when I am working on a rough dummy, but it's there in the back of my mind somewhere.

Films have always been a source of inspiration. I like the black-and-white ones best, especially old comedies with great masters like Buster Keaton and Harold Lloyd. Also moody Hollywood dramas of the '30s and '40s. The cinema represented Glamour in the genteel seaside town on the Wirral, near Liverpool, where I grew up, most especially during the war – a rather grey dreary time. We fought our way in the blackout down the cold windy promenade to every available performance. If the siren went the projectionist played the same film round again until the all-clear. Any fear of a direct hit was far outweighed by the pleasure of getting a free second showing. I find that I still retain whole passages of the dialogue by heart – rather frustrating when I think of all the chunks of Shakespeare and Milton which now elude me.

We were an all-female household, three daughters and a widowed mother. I was the youngest. It was a contented enough childhood, but very sheltered. The social round was non-existent. There was ample time for messing about, unsupervised by grown-ups. To combat boredom we wrote stories and illustrated them, got up magazines, dressed up, made up plays and acted them to anyone we could press into service as an audience. I think I have always depended upon writing and drawing as a reliable bastion against boredom or loneliness. I suppose there was also a lurking Welsh desire to show off, to burst out from behind the sitting-room curtains hoping for applause.

I read a lot, or rather mooned about over books, re-reading the same old favourites – *Milly Molly Mandy*, the *William* books, *The Wind in the Willows*, *Mary Plain* – over and over. The pictures were always fascinating, especially classics with illustrations by Rackham, Dulac and Heath Robinson. They had line drawings set into the text and tipped-in colour plates on a special high-gloss paper. Christmas annuals – *Pip, Squeak and Wilfred* and *Tiger Tim* were a perennial pleasure. Once, when I had measles, a lady gave me a huge collection of old American comics (the 'Funnies') which had an electrifying effect. The content and style of drawing was something I had never seen before. I spent a lot of time pouring over *Lil' Abner*, *Little Orphan Annie*, George McManus's *Bringing Up Father* and the great Winsor McCay's *Little Nemo*, and trying to copy the different styles.

I kept on drawing. There was always some narrative

connection. I certainly wasn't discouraged at home and at school it was the only thing that I was any good at. At sixteen I got to Liverpool Art School to study costume design. But there was never any serious thought that art could be a profession – it was more a way of filling in time before getting married. Some years later, after completing a course at the Ruskin School of Fine Art at Oxford, I wrote to a distinguished publisher and typographer asking for advice on how to become an illustrator of children's books. He replied in more or less the same terms, saying that such an endeavour would be out of the question 'except as an adjunct to teaching or matrimony'.

Nevertheless I had made up my mind to be one. After a long haul of doing the rounds with a folio I managed to get some work illustrating run-of-the-mill children's books. You did between twelve and twenty line drawings and a full-colour jacket. Children's fiction was very bracing and outgoing in those days, with plenty of romping about on ponies and camping out. The pay was meagre. But I gradually graduated to illustrating some really good authors – Noel Streatfield, Dorothy Edwards, the young William Mayne. And fairy tales. It was excellent practice, and helped me to pluck up courage to write something of my own.

It was a publisher (Victor Gollancz) who, knowing my work as an illustrator, first suggested that I should try to write my own picture book. I wrote the simplest story I could think of for very young children (I had two of my own by then). It was called *Lucy and Tom's Day*. So the move from being a working illustrator, which I hope I still am, to an author had begun.

I think that ever since, as a child, I gazed at those sumptuous Victorian narrative paintings in the Walker Art Gallery in Liverpool and the Port Sunlight Collection, works with titles like *Samson* and *When Did You Last See Your Father?*, I have felt strongly that pictures and stories belong together. I suspect that a good many other children out there feel the same way.

MICHAEL ROSEN

Writer, poet, performer, broadcaster and scriptwriter, Michael Rosen has been writing for children of all ages since 1970. He has talked to children, parents and teachers all over Britain, Australia, Canada and Singapore. His work is translated into Japanese, German, French, Spanish and Dutch. Born in 1946, he lives in London with his wife and five children and spends his time writing, visiting schools, doing television and radio programmes and shopping. He has regularly presented the children's book programme, *Treasure Islands* on BBC Radio 4. Michael Rosen is currently studying for an MA in Children's Literature at Reading University and is working on *An Anthology of Childhood*.

Previous titles include:

Under the Bed – The Bedtime Book

Smelly Jelly, Smelly Fish – The Seaside Book

Hard-Boiled Legs – The Breakfast Book

Spollyollydiddlytiddlyitis – The Doctor Book

Did I Hear You Write?

The Hypnotiser

Who Drew on the Baby's Head?

The Golem of Old Prague

Mind the Gap and Other Poems

Action Replay

Burping Bertha

Little Red Riding Pudd

MICHAEL ROSEN

An Anarchist in the Rhododendrons

Writing for children is marginal. Anyone doing it has to be cheery and resolute about its status, roughly equivalent to the kind of books you see in the 'Humour' sections of bookshops. Books for children are often seen as ephemeral, Christmassy, fill-in-a-bit-of-time sort of stuff. Anyone involved in the business knows that look you get from childless intellectuals when you say, 'children's books' – a look that spells out trivial, demeaning, frivolous and ultimately beneath seriousness. In trying to suggest otherwise, it is easy to be caught in a double bind. No, you might say, children's literature addresses serious, contemporary themes, thereby conceding that to be a good entertainer like Martin Handford and his *Where's Wally* books is somehow less important than producing a novel about Time. It's a concession that must never be made. To be able to engage the interest of millions of people of any age is a huge achievement and has to be taken seriously if only because it tells us something about ourselves, our behaviour and our minds.

It's children's fault. Perhaps children's literature is unimportant because children are unimportant. Our culture sees children as small creatures hanging around waiting to be grown-up. Millions of pounds have been spent writing, peddling and enforcing a National Curriculum that is based on a model of development similar to that of Ford cars. The child arrives at school incomplete and raw and is subjected to various processes over the next eleven years that will render it complete and saleable. Each addition to the frame can be observed and assessed as if it were an object and, as the frame passes on to the next process, each object can be assumed to have stayed, stuck to the frame. Sadly, this bears little relation to how learning actually takes place, which must always treat the learner as an active component in the process – not as an object that passively receives lumps of knowledge.

In the popular sphere, children appear alternatively as clothes-hangers, consumers, victims or appendages. Think of how children appear in advertisements, as 'news', or in films and TV soaps. Count the number of times you see on adult TV or in the newspapers, children structuring their own perceptions of the world, their friends or their family. It seems to be vital for our culture both in education and in the mass media to see children as passive. So to say, as I did, that children's literature might be unimportant because children are unimportant is wrong. Children's literature is unimportant because children are important. We need to have a model of ourselves as adults at some kind of pinnacle of development, rather like notions of the development of civilisation itself, slowly rising to perfection in . . . 1994? 2001? and the Holocaust, mass unemployment or Third World starvation are just blips on a beautiful rising curve. In a society dominated by notions of hierarchy, classes, command structures, and differentially distributed wealth, we reproduce the same notions in our attitudes to children. Every day we remind ourselves that children are stupid, not doing well enough, petty, trivial, facetious and, yes, childish. Unlike adults who do grown-up things like go to war, sack miners, pollute Shetland and abuse children.

So children's literature enters a world that is actively structuring perceptions of children. It is not separate from it but twists and turns about, sometimes confirming, sometimes defying these perceptions. It wriggles about between 'how-adults-perceive-children' and 'how-children-perceive-adults'. Now this is interesting stuff. Take any children's book, past or present, and ask yourself these questions: what is this saying to children about adults? What is this saying to children about children? What is this saying to adults about children? What is this saying to adults about adults? Do the answers converge or diverge? Take the *William* books. William is an anarchist in a middle-class world of maids, drawing-rooms and rhododendron bushes. We might say, how much on the side of the child, Richmal Crompton was, or, they are satires of English commuter-belt life of the 1920s . . . But then why is the prose entirely composed of elaborate put-downs? William's activities are diminished by high-flown language: 'The colour of William's tongue would have put to shame Spring's freshest tints'. Who is this funny for? What is the joke here? As I said, children's literature twists and turns between two poles. When Robert Louis Stevenson wrote *A Child's Garden of Verses* one of his first critics complained that the poems weren't sufficiently appealing to an adult sense of humour which, for children's literature to be really good, should be concealed from the child.

When I first started writing poetry I wrote imitations of D. H. Lawrence, moved on to imitations of Gerard Manley Hopkins and then happened on what I thought were imitations of Carl Sandburg, e e cummings and the opening chapters of James Joyce's *Portrait of an Artist*. How pretentious can you get! But then I was twenty or so. I think what I thought I was doing was writing about my childhood, for adults, in the voice of a child. As it happens the only people who seemed to be interested in this were people who were on the look out for poetry for children, from anywhere – British and Irish folk song, Ancient Chinese poetry, oral poetry from anywhere, accessible snippets of classics from Shakespeare to T. S. Eliot and so on. A child audience was found for me. I entered the institution of schools, children's book groups, book fairs, children's libraries and children's and schools' TV and radio.

I had experienced an adult audience for my writing through having had a play of mine put on at the Royal Court in London. It had been a dispiriting time. The audience seemed to be some kind of élite. I couldn't justify to myself why I was limiting what I was writing to one small section of the population. Whether this came from a humanistic, socialistic or just naïve frame of mind, I'm not absolutely sure. But looking back at myself then (I was about twenty-one) I'm not ashamed of the idea that I thought it was important to find a popular audience – or to put it another way: if you have anything important to say, then it should be said in such a way that most people can get hold of it, or it won't be important.

So I found a popular audience, albeit often coralled in classrooms. I arrived at schools and performed poems, anecdotes, juggling, stories, funny faces to hundreds and thousands of children. I started doing workshops with children where I would ask them to write and perform. I started making contact with children in a variety of ways, me as adult reflecting on my childhood, the children reflecting on their childhood, me as adult reflecting on my own children's lives, me as adult reflecting on how I relate to my children as a parent, the children reflecting on how they relate to parents, and all adults . . . and so on. From what started out as a rather literary preoccupation with expressing autobiographical ideas, I had met children's culture face to face.

Rather strangely this coincided with hostile reviewing from critics. I started getting criticism that complained that what I was writing was 'not poetry'. I started getting the impression that there was a school of thought that my becoming popular was a bad thing. I had sown weeds in the garden of poetry. I had cheapened the word 'poetry' because I was 'cavalier' with form, I wrote large 'shapeless' chunks of chopped-up prose. I learnt that Sandy Brownjohn, widely acclaimed for her books on children's own writing, had banned my books from her school. Wow!

I now realised that in some circles feelings ran very high about 'literary merit' and children; that there was a body of thought and opinion that imported arguments about 'great literature', the canon and the heritage from the adult sphere into the children's. I saw it as a rather pathetic guying of all that was bad about my Oxford University English course with its view of literature as some kind of baton-changing of greatness down the centuries, where the process of literary production was seen as simply one great writer influencing another. It was that peculiar, stiff upper-lip refusal to include notions of audience, society and ideology into considerations of literature. In a rather mistaken way, I had imagined that I had kept my social-critical activities confined to the political sphere but I now discovered, to my surprise, that rather than these poems and stories about my childhood being non-political or less political, they were in fact seen as just as subversive as taking part in a demonstration or supporting a strike.

All this has suddenly become of acute relevance. It has long been a legend put about by the literary heritage mob that nasty left-wing people hanging about in cultural studies departments of polytechnics (as were) had ruined literature by politicising it with all their talk of ideology and theory. Now, this government will stipulate what children read. We now have texts with government-approval stamps on them. In January 1993, the National Curriculum Council produced a list of 144 examples (by author or book) of approved literature some of which would have to be read and some of which should be read. What a historic moment! It was an attempt to gain more ideological control over children, teachers and parents than had ever been attempted before. After all, even with near-compulsory Christian education in schools, it was never stipulated exactly which parts of the Bible had to be covered. Because I attended two different primary schools assemblies changed from sermons from an Old Testament hell-fire preacher to ones from a New Testament evangelist. What dangerous pluralism that now looks. Children at Key Stage 2 (!) should read two of the following: *Alice, Peter Pan, Just William, Swallows and Amazons, Wind in the Willows, The Lion, the Witch and the Wardrobe, Winnie the Pooh, The Jungle Book, The Railway Children, The Little House on the Prairie* and *What Katy Did.*

These books are so good, so fine in their presentation of universal values – presumably including notions of common humanity, freedom of speech, human rights and duties, human mortality in the face of God, infinity and the universe etc etc – that we will make you, force you to read them. It will not be necessary for us to justify intellectually why these books are great; we will not attempt to convince you by reason, example, emotion or science that they should be read. Simply, you will read them. And 'we' are the government, 'we' are the law and cannot be defied. What finer example could you have of the politicisation of literature, a degrading of literature in the interests of power, control and containment. It shows a contempt for children, teachers and parents, that between us we can decide what we should read and how. In that sense, in the midst of its dictatorial exercise of power, it shows a certain nervousness: the people cannot be trusted. And they're right. The people can never be trusted to accept the ruthless wielding of power. In hundreds of small ways, and perhaps in big ways too, people will assert their right to have more control over their own lives.

So children are very important. Their minds must be structured by what the government thinks is great literature. It is a crude attempt to redefine nationality at the very moment that it is under threat with an imploding monarchy and an exploding sovereignty. In the face of this assault, the institution of children's literature with its chatty sharing of books, its informality, its jokes, its rudenesses, its ephemerality, its ruthless pursuit of pleasure is delightfully dangerous. I celebrate its marginality.

The Writer's World

Illustration by Ann Ross Paterson

MAYA ANGELOU

Singer, actress, dancer and black activist, Maya Angelou is one of America's finest and most popular contemporary writers. Born in St Louis, Missouri, she grew up in Arkansas and in California, where she became the first black person to work on the streetcars. At the age of sixteen, she gave birth to her son Guy, and in her twenties she toured Europe and Africa as principal dancer in *Porgy and Bess*. On her return to America, she moved to New York, joined the Harlem Writers Guild and continued to earn a living as a nightclub singer and performer. She also appeared in the television series, *Roots*. In the 1960s, active in black politics, she worked with Martin Luther King in the Southern Christian Leadership Conference and later spent several years in Ghana as editor of the *African Review*.

Since *I Know Why the Caged Bird Sings* was first published in 1984, Maya Angelou has become a celebrity in Britain, talking and performing to packed audiences. The story of her extraordinary life now runs to five volumes.

Previous titles include:

*I Know Why the Caged
   Bird Sings*
Gather Together in My Name
*Singin' and Swingin' and Gettin'
   Merry like Christmas*
The Heart of a Woman
*All God's Children Need
   Travelling Shoes*

And I Still Rise
*Now Sheba Sings the
   Song*
*Just Give Me a Cool Drink
   of Water*
*Oh, Pray My Wings are
   Gonna Fit Me Well*

MAYA ANGELOU

On . . .

On Hats

I rarely wear hats but I met a writer, a television personality and presenter named Midge McKenzie, who's a tall English woman. She affects hats, she has hats, and when you see her you want to ask, 'Hat, bring that girl back here.' Well, I saw her about three weeks ago and then last week I went back to San Francisco for a minute to see my parents, my mom and son, and I passed a store and there was this hat and I knew I was going to do Meet The Author in Edinburgh and I thought this is the thing to do, buy that hat. Affect it. You know you don't wear this kind of hat, you affect that. And then on Wednesday morning when I sat in front of readers I will wear the hat and even if I make no sense at all in anything I say, something about the hat makes you think *that* is an authority.

On Roots

I think there is that in the human spirit which needs to go home. We romanticise home. Sometimes that's what we are purportedly looking for when we go to the Canary Islands. Really, what we are looking for is some identification, some place where we really feel great. Thomas Wolfe was right in the title of his book, *You Can't Go Home Again*. But he was also wrong, because in truth, you can never leave home, you take it with you. It is under the fingernails, it's in the hair follicles, it's in the bends of the elbows, it's behind the knee-caps; home is always there. It's in the way you walk, you know, it's in the droop of the shoulders, it's in our fear, in our courage, the demons of childhood remain with us, in forming sometimes the way we were able to say good morning or unable to say good morning. So this title of my book, *All God's Children Need Travelling Shoes*, I take that from the fact that a number of people reach positions, they get titles, they get names, I mean they get positions, they become the greatest of the great. They marry *the* woman or *the* man, to have *the* two and a half children, you know, and move into *the* block of flats or *the* house, get *the* car and then they start to think, oh, I've got it now. I belong to *the* club, I belong to *the* church, or *the* temple or *the* synagogue or something. I've got *it*. I've got my head the right colour now. Fantastic! And then they think they have stopped but the truth is they should keep on their travelling shoes because we are all in process, every one of us.

I had always been suspicious of people who would come back, black Americans in particular, who would come to Ghana and say, 'I know I'm Ghanti,' or 'I know I'm Ashanti,' or they go to Nigeria, 'I know I'm Nigerian,' 'I know I'm Polimi.' Well, the truth is, if they are black Americans, more I suppose, than anyone else, or any other Africans in the diaspora, our people were not allowed to be together. When a slave ship would come in with a load of crew or scientific people, our people were split up immediately so they could not speak the language. It was suggested by the American slavers that if people spoke the same language, they could form a revolution. We were obliged to speak English immediately. That was the only lingan, I mean that was the only language. People inter-married and as slaves were not allowed to inter-marry and truth was, they inter-bred. They bred with other tribes and the black American is the perfect example of the Pan African. It shows that all those tribes could come together. For a black American to go back to Africa and say, I know I am a part of this, well he is probably that and seven others, you know?

On Reading

I had the good fortune with my son to have literature. So I could be the mother and the strong fella on the other side but I also had literature on that other side and I conked it into him. By the time he was four, I told him he had to read. I didn't know that he had to, but he was boring me when *I* was reading. So I told him, 'If you learn to read you're going to love it.' Not only does literature entertain and amuse, it really informs. It educates us and as that is one of the rules, naturally of the mother, but also of the father, I let literature do that for me. I was very blessed and if I have a monument in the world, my son is my monument.

On Writing

It's as easy reading as it is damn hard writing. And that's an understatement. I keep a hotel room in the town where I live and I leave my house about a quarter to six every morning. I go to the hotel room. I don't have anything on the walls – I have them take everything off the walls. I keep a bible, a dictionary, Roget's Thesaurus, a bottle of sherry and a deck of cards and I go in there and I work. I work until about 12.30. If the work is going very well, I will work until half-past one and then I go home because writing is very hard work. Then I put on some slacks or an easy skirt and I go shopping and pretend to be normal, speak to people, and come home and cook. After I eat, I look at the work I did that day and try to edit it. I go to sleep and then go to work the next morning.

It takes about a year and a half to write a book. I ask myself all the time why I do it. But I know I am a writer. I've made a living doing a lot of things, but writing is the only thing I've ever loved and the only area in which I have a chance to be what I am here to be. To inform, to entertain, to express myself. I loved to dance when I was young. That's the only other thing I loved but my knees are very, very bad and early on, I had an affliction which prohibited me ever becoming a great dancer. I can sing but I will never be a great singer because I don't love it enough. I'm not willing to make sacrifices for it.

On Autobiography

I decided, when I chose to write my autobiography, that I would try to tell the truth, not necessarily just the facts, because facts can obscure the truth. You can tell so many facts that nobody understands, nobody gives a damn. But I also decided that, while I would tell the truth, I didn't have to tell everything I know. So I try to be selective and write in a sort of broad 'every man, woman' theme. I deal with honesty, deal with friendship, deal with generosity, deal with greed, deal with unkindness, narrowness, meanness of spirit. Deal with those large human issues. That means then if I am successful in writing about one black girl or one black woman, an Asian woman in Tapei will read it and say, 'That's the truth.' A middle-class white woman in Dorset will read it and say, 'That's the truth.' Somebody in Aberdeen will read it and say, 'That's the truth.' It happened to this girl in St Louis, Missouri, or this woman in San Francisco, says the tall black woman, I understand it. A white man in Stockholm reads it and says, 'That's the truth.' And so I'm talking about the black experience and that's why I know. But I'm always talking about the human condition, about what it is like to be a human being, about what makes us weep and wail and cry and fall and feel and then rise.

On Influences

When I was growing up I read what was available to me, and what was available were books from the white school which had been thrown away. The spines were gone, the glue in the spine had been eaten and so we had to get the books and re-bind them, make glue out of flour and water and put those books back together, get cardboard, make backs for them and fronts and then cover that with cardboard and brown paper. What I read first were Dickens, Poe, Shakespeare and those restored books and they were as valuable to me as anything I have ever had later because they helped me to learn this language. Now there was, I'm happy to say, a group of black women poets in the nineteenth century who meant the earth to me too, but I didn't meet them until I was about fourteen.

On Fate

I think a lot of what we do can be credited to fate – I do believe that. If you hadn't gone to that party you wouldn't have met so and so who became your husband and then he became the father of the children and blah blah blah. Had you turned right instead of turning left you wouldn't have run into the friend who said, 'Listen Bill . . . ' and met a whole new group of people and so on. I do believe that you should try to stay in a state of grace, and I mean that religiously. This is to say, to be ready to listen to life. Life loves a liver of it. It shows you that we will all die, that is the only promise we can be sure of. This is the most scary thing and yet the only one we know we will do. If we can do that, then it seems to me that we can attempt other things – everything else is less than that! So we can attempt to write better, to live better, to be stronger, funnier and more generous, learn to cry harder. My grandmother used to tell me when I cried, she said, 'Sister, don't cry, because the more you cry, the less you pee, and peeing is much more important.' I believed it.

On Men and Friendship

What we need among ourselves between women and men, and men and men, and women and women, is friendship. We desperately need it. Any one of us, given the luck and the inclination, can find sex, so that is not what we're asking. That is not what is really the cry in the middle of our bellies, in the middle of our hearts. We are crying and desperately in need of friendship, and men are excellent when they become good friends, and women are excellent, too.

On Achieving Years

I wanted to become older. I didn't know what all that meant. I thought I would become older and look the same. I didn't know it meant my hair would turn a different colour and all the bones ache. I look reasonably young for my age but the bones will not let you forget, not for a minute. I didn't know it meant sagging muscles and thickening waists, I didn't know that. But I take that, it goes with the territory. So it's all right, I feel good and cheerful. I don't say I feel good all the time but I'm usually cheerful and I have a wonderful capacity for White Label Scotch, which is a blessing!

From a 'Meet the Author' event chaired by Sheena McDonald,
at the 1987 Festival

CLAUDIA RODEN

Claudia Roden was born and brought up in Cairo. She finished her education in Paris and then moved to London to study art. Since her childhood, she has travelled extensively throughout the Mediterranean. Starting as a painter, she was drawn to the subject of food partly as a desire to evoke a lost heritage – one of the pleasures of a happy life in Egypt. Her bestselling classic, *A Book of Middle Eastern Food*, was first published in 1968. She has continued to write about food, with a special interest in the social and historical background of cooking. She was married to an Englishman and has three grown-up children.

Previous titles include:

A New Book of Middle Eastern Food

Coffee

Picnic – the Complete Guide to Outdoor Food

Sainsbury's Middle Eastern Cooking

Mediterranean Cookery

The Food of Italy

CLAUDIA RODEN

Holding on to a Vanished World

To be a writer never entered my mind when I was a child. The image of a writer presented by my mother in Egypt was of a man of extreme egoism who sacrificed his family because, as he was constantly repeating: *'le geni doit survivre!'* A writer was the opposite of what a woman should be – the 'sunshine' of the family, ever present, concerned and solicitous, offering hospitality, succour and sustenance to those around her.

Egyptian Jews talked a great deal but never wrote. Every gathering, however large or small, became a fight to be heard. People shouted across the room and across conversations. Their talk was so animated that outsiders might think they were engaged in a violent quarrel. Everyone had something to say about everything and everybody. Women especially, whose main activity was visiting, amassed a gigantic fund of information and stories. They had every family history at their fingertips and they could even repeat word-for-word conversations at which they had not been present. There was no need and no time to write and nobody wanted to spend any time alone to do so. Being alone was considered horrible and something to be ashamed of. And there was no tradition of writing.

I recently discovered a book about the Jews of Egypt in the nineteenth century which contained a letter by my great-grandfather. He was a teacher at the Alliance Israelite Française in Istanbul and was sent to assess the possibility of opening schools in Egypt. (The Alliance was a charitable institution which brought French to the Jewish communities in the Middle East which were seen to be in intellectual decline.) He wrote back that the children spoke six languages but could not read or write (boys were taught Hebrew parrot-like) and he doubted that they could be made to sit down in a class.

In my days we spoke French (with an unorthodox grammar and our own special intonation) and a peculiar Italian with a smattering of Judeo-Spanish and English at school. My paternal grandparents spoke Arabic. We moved from one language to another in our speech which was infected by all the jargons of the Levant and reinforced by gesticulations and facial expressions. I passed my English GCE exams and went on to take my Baccalaureate in Paris but I remained with the idea that I knew none of the languages properly, let alone enough to write them.

I did not think of my first book – *A Book of Middle Eastern Food* – as writing. Cookery books were not considered so twenty–six years ago. But still, for me, collecting recipes was a matter of urgency and a labour charged with emotion. Each recipe represented a precious discovery, a way of holding on to a vanished world and of recreating a happy past that was lost.

In 1956, when I was studying art in London, my parents had to leave Egypt as a result of the Suez intervention and the traumas of the war with Israel. Ten years on most of the once large and very ancient Jewish community had disappeared and my life was engulfed in a sea of exiles. In those days I was married with three young children and living in London, but it seemed as though Egypt was all around me with friends and relatives stopping over on their way to a new country. My parents' Friday night dinners became legendary. We had been a society that cared about food and it was one of the things we missed most. Everyone talked about food and exchanged recipes. In Egypt we had not used books nor were there any published recipes. The most precious gift we could give, it seemed, was a recipe. People got them from acquaintances met in a cinema queue or at an airport, and proudly passed them on.

I started tracking down people who had reputations for good cooking and wrote all over the world for recipes. In Egypt nobody would have given them. Now that we were dispersed, the old jealous competitiveness disappeared and everyone was eager to be generous. I could not talk to anyone without asking them to describe a dish and such things as whether they fried or used batter or flour or bread-crumbs. I must have been a terrible bore. But I was obsessed and insatiable like a crazed collector. In the end, because our community had not been homogeneous and was made up of families from Turkey, North Africa, Syria and other Middle Eastern countries, I went on to cover almost all of them.

In those days there were none of the cookery books that are around now, and most of my information had to come from people. Collecting recipes was an occasion to chat about their lives and to hear their stories and some of that went into the book with the recipes. I wrote mostly in French and when I had tested the recipes and amended them (they didn't always come right), I re-wrote them in English on the kitchen table.

Apart fom providing our everyday meals, the book was an important part of my life. It was meant to be a one-off exercise. I never intended to make a career of cookery writing. But it started me off using words, which I enjoyed, and I became addicted to the subject of food. I hate being isolated and sitting down writing for hours (now I use a word processor) but I adore the research, seeing people connected with food, talking about it, cooking and eating. It is a sensuous field that deals with pleasure and I like that. Cooking is an art that is open to everybody and the result is for the enjoyment of others. I am gregarious by nature and people involved in food are usually good to be with. To me writing about food does not stop at the saucepan or the plate. It is an occasion to write about people and their world. It also allows you to try to be the 'sunshine' of the family by feeding them well.

DERVLA MURPHY

Dervla Murphy was born of Dublin parents in 1931 in County Waterford. From childhood her wish was to write and to travel. At the age of fourteen, she had to leave school to look after her invalid mother, but she continued her education by reading widely and cycling in Europe. After her mother's death in 1962, she cycled to India and worked with Tibetan refugees before returning home to write her first two books. Her next journeys were to Nepal and to Ethiopia; then the birth of her daughter Rachel, in December 1968, put a temporary stop to adventuring.

In 1973 she and Rachel set off on their first long journey together, through South India. A year later, they trekked through the Karakoram with an ex-polo pony and, in 1978, walked 1,300 miles through the Peruvian Andes with a pack-mule. Dervla Murphy has also written about the conflict in Northern Ireland and about the nuclear controversy. To date, she has written sixteen books. Her most recent, *The Ukimwi Road* is published in autumn 1993.

WRITERS WRITING

Previous titles include:

Full Tilt: Ireland to India with
  a Bicycle
The Waiting Land: A Spell
  in Nepal
In Ethiopia with a Mule
On a Shoestring in Coorg:
  An Experience of South India
Where the Indus is Young:
  A Winter in Baltisan
A Place Apart: Northern
  Ireland

Wheels Within Wheels:
  Autobiography
Race to the Finish?:
  The Nuclear Stakes
Eight Feet in the Andes
Muddling Through in
  Madagascar
Tales from Two Cities:
  Travel of Another Sort
Cameroon with Egbert
Transylvania and beyond

DERVLA MURPHY

Stray Thoughts

There are, I'm told, obscure American universities which collect the original typescripts and manuscripts of minor contemporary authors, presumably because they can't afford to run in the Waugh/Auden stakes. My publisher once suggested that for this reason I should cherish my own typescripts and manuscripts, instead of using them to light the fire. (I don't buy newspapers; the BBC tells me all I want to know about world affairs – no pun intended.) One distant day, Jock Murray said, my daughter might be able to turn an honest cent by flogging the Papers of Dervla Murphy, especially as books first written out in long-hand are rapidly acquiring scarcity value. This kindly suggestion made me shudder and blush: an illogical reaction since we're considering the post-mortem era. However, my skeleton would undoubtedly rattle with shame should anyone – but *anyone* – ever see the humiliating mess that is Draft One and Two of a D. M. book. Not until Draft Three does it begin to look something other than the scribblings of a person with learning difficulties. Then slowly and painfully it pulls itself together and Draft Four (or so) becomes publishable.

Contemplating the scribbled welter of clichés, truisms, irrelevancies, incoherencies, superfluous adjectives, passages purple or bloated and syntax hideously contorted – contemplating this unpromising embryo I envy all those other

157

writers whose well-disciplined minds subdue this chaos *before* they put pen to paper (or finger to key). I have to make the mess before clearing it up – well, more or less clearing it up. This is why it takes me so long to produce the sort of book that anyone else could throw off in a month or two. It's hard work but I suppose I enjoy it or I would have spent the past thirty years doing something else. But stay! *What* else! There is nothing else I can do . . . That however just could be because I never wanted to do anything else, which simplifies life from the start: in my case from Year Five, though my first book was not published until Year Thirty-Two. Entitled *Full Tilt*, it described my experiences while cycling to India in 1963. Meanwhile I had written at least six full-length unpublished books and accumulated a mound of rejection slips that might have daunted anyone less certain of what they wanted to do with their life.

Thirty years ago my sort of travelling lacked glamour and the media felt no compulsion to probe travellers' motives. As I quietly prepared to cycle from Ireland to India nobody thought to ask me if I were going on this journey in order to celebrate feminine autonomy, or to get my own country in perspective, or to escape from a society in which I felt a misfit or to acquire heroic standing in the public eye. People merely concluded that I was crazy and made no further comment. Effortless mass-tourism had recently burgeoned and sane folk flew to India, quite cheaply, in eight hours.

Therefore I set off happily, in January 1963, unaware of the need for either a convoluted hidden motive or a serious purpose. I did, of course, have a frivolous purpose: to enjoy myself. I had been looking forward to this adventure since the age of ten, when I decided to cycle to India – eventually, in adulthood. Now it is clear that that decision – which even then was a firm *decision*, not a childhood whim – fore-shadowed the structure of most of my future journeys. Although I was to become a professional writer, I have remained an amateur traveller. By temperament I am interested only in journeys that may be undertaken alone (or, during her childhood, with my daughter), unshackled by media subsidies or publishers' commissions, independent of new-fangled equipment and free of intrusive publicity. A certain amount of publicity is, of course, inevitable when books are being launched; but that martyrdom to modern marketing comes long after the journey and fails to taint it. The travel writer's emphasis shifts, I have found, as one ages. When cycling to India, or walking across the Ethiopian Highlands twenty-five years ago, the journey – *my* journey – was the most important thing. My testing of myself, my observations and reactions, my failures or achievements – it was all, I now realise, deplorably egocentric. Of course the local people mattered, both for their own sakes and for mine. When travelling alone in places like the Simien Mountains or, the Karakoum you don't survive unless you can establish a genuine rapport with the locals. However, they and their problems were secondary to my personal fulfilment through adventure. Certainly I never thought of the subsequent book as 'having a message' or 'informing'; my task – and pleasure – was to share the fun I had had with my readers.

Gradually that changed, I think, while I was writing non-travel books – about Northern Ireland's problems, the nuclear power industry (undesirability of) and race relations in Britain. The extent and nature of the change only recently became apparent to me, when I cycled (in March–June 1992) from Nairobi to Zimbabwe via Uganda, Tanzania, Malawi and Zambia. Over much of the way Africa's roads made the advertisements of mountain-bike manufacturers seem less than accurate and for me as a traveller this journey's challenges – the exhilarating unpredictability of it all – provided no less fun than that cycle to India all those years ago. Yet for me as a writer the pendulum had swung. Back home, in July, settling down to write *The Ukimwi Road*, I did have a message. My energies were being expended not so much on describing landscapes or personal experiences as on trying to convey how grave and urgent are Africa's crises – and how disastrously we whites are compounding many problems by continuing to meddle for our own (direct or indirect) profit. Several other writers have done this, and done it far better than I can; but there is a compulsion, now, to contribute my mite. Probably this will be bad for sales; there is no discernible public out there ravening for depressing books about Africa. But contrary to popular opinion, sales are not uppermost in the average writer's mind: were money-making the name of the game, we would be an exceedingly depressed species. (Apart from the minority who get – and sometimes deserve – six-figure advances.)

The compensation for not being rich is being free. What other job leaves the worker so in control of his or her own life? Painting, sculpting and composing, perhaps? Yet not really; those artists have to tangle with what seems to me the intimidating commercial side of their activities: seeking commissions, hiring galleries for exhibitions, arranging for the performance or recording of a new composition. In contrast, writers only have to finish a book, parcel up the typescript, send it off to a publisher, correct the proofs and get on with the next book – leaving the publisher with the formidable task of persuading an unenthusiastic public that out of those 60,000-odd books now appearing annually in Britain, *this* is the one on which an outrageous amount of money should be spent.

Or am I over-simplifying? Are John Murray authors luckier than most in the 1990s? One does hear frequent horror stories from fellow authors about books commissioned and then rejected, some take-over having gone sour; about editors evaporating overnight and their successors being uninterested in the work-in-progress; about sales managers who couldn't sell ice-cream in a heat-wave; about typescripts being mangled to fit house-styles; about agents who insist that an author's only way forward is to drag a supermarket trolley across the Gobi Desert (preferably trailed by a TV crew), or to write a 650-page novel featuring a manic depressive nymphomaniac infiltrating the Bank of England's Board of Directors. Is this now the real world, from which John Murray authors are protected within the eighteenth-century fastness of No. 50 Albemarle Street? If it is, I want to stay well away from it. Murrays have never commissioned a book: *I* decide what I want to write about. I have never had an agent: given a mutually happy and trusting publisher-author relationship, agents are a pointless extravagance – and a potential threat to the individual author's independence.

Naturally there is a price to be paid for all this independence. Once has to organise oneself, to spur oneself on, to develop and stick with a routine. For travel books, the recommended (by me) routine is to start work immediately on returning home, not allowing extraneous concerns or interests to blur the impact of the journey. This isn't always possible; I returned from Madagascar with Hepatitis A which atrophied my brain for six months. (Some readers of *Muddling Through in Madagascar* reckon it was atrophied for much longer.) And within a day of returning from Cameroon I picked up a London virus which eventually became pericarditis – and on getting home from my second tour of Romania I found the drains blocked in a macabre and time-consuming way. But on more fortunate occasions I at once isolate myself (gates locked; telephone off the hook; post unopened) by way of remaining, mentally, in the relevant and now remote country. This device works so well that I'm sometimes surprised, after several hours' work, to realise that I am in fact in Ireland.

In my case inspiration never comes so one doesn't sit around waiting for it, as one might be tempted to do were it an occasional visitor. There are, however, stratagems for overcoming this lack. On retiring at 9.30p.m., I never leave a blank page to be faced at 5.30a.m. That way lies madness, or at best despair. There must be something, however feeble, on the post-breakfast page – indeed, its very feebleness can be the stimulus that sets the literary adrenaline flowing. And if on some rare morning it isn't feeble, but vaguely hopeful, one goes off like a rocket and that will be a *good* day . . .

Travel writers, confronting 'page 1, Chapter One', have the advantage of not starting from scratch. To hand lies one's journal, much longer than the book will be, recording many details and conversations and impressions superfluous to the finished product though well worth the labour of noting down each evening. Those stained and battered notebooks, still faintly smelling of leaked kerosene and trapped wood-smoke, are the essential quarry from which a travel book is mined. Keeping one's journal up-to-date is a genuine stamina test; at the end of a long day's walking or cycling, there is no eagerness to put pen to paper. Food and sleep are the instinctive priorities, yet not to write is fatal; one day's observations and encounters are too easily blurred by the next day's. And, while conversations, impressions and observations may be deliberately merged in the book, they must be kept distinct in the journal; this ensures that their individual significance is clear, back home, and merging can be done without distortion. According to my old-fashioned ideas, travel writing is more akin to responsible journalism than to creative writing and even in my early books I always felt an obligation to report accurately – and as objectively as possible. The result may not be very exciting, but as Byron once noted,

'Tis pleasant, sure, to see one's name in print;
A book's a book, although there's nothing in 't.

Background to Writing

Illustration by Albert Uderzo

MARGARET FORSTER

Margaret Forster was born in Carlisle in 1938. She was educated there at the County High School and won an Open Scholarship to Somerville College, Oxford, where, in 1960, she was awarded an honours degree in History. In the same year, she married Hunter Davies.

Since 1963 she has worked as a novelist, biographer and freelance literary critic, contributing regularly to book programmes on television, BBC Radio 4 and to various newspapers and magazines. She has written seventeen novels and was shortlisted for the *Sunday Express* Book of the Year Award in 1989. She has also published a number of biographies, including *Elizabeth Barrett Browning* which won the Royal Society of Literature Award for 1988, and *Daphne du Maurier*. Her novel *Lady's Maid* was based on the life of Wilson, lady's maid to Elizabeth Barrett Browning. Margaret Forster lives with her husband in London and Loweswater. They have three children.

Previous titles include:

Mother Can You Hear Me?	*Elizabeth Barrett Browning*
Private Papers	*Have the Men had Enough?*
Georgy Girl	*Lady's Maid*
The Rash Adventurer	*The Battle for Christabel*
Significant Sisters	*Daphne du Maurier*

MARGARET FORSTER

On the Delicate Art of Contemporary Biography

There is no doubt it has been a shock. When I moved from fiction to biography in the first place, I was startled to discover that, in spite of a degree in History, I'd all too obviously left Oxford without the faintest idea of how to do any proper research, but I didn't expect to find that attempting to write the biography of someone who had just died would be so radically different from writing one about someone long dead. I'm afraid it is like learning a new language.

To start with, the subject of the biography may be dead but a great many of their family and friends will be alive. What joy that thought initially caused me – how wonderful, I thought, if I'd been able to talk to Elizabeth Barrett Browning's sister or to her son or, especially, to her servants, so many questions would be answered, so many mysteries solved. How naïve I was. The moment I began meeting Daphne du Maurier's circle I realised I was completely out of my depth.

Here I had a significant number of people all of whom had known Daphne intimately and had so much to tell. All it needed, surely, was for me to get them started and out it would all pour. But not a bit of it. Nothing poured, it trickled. It trickled and it stopped until I learned how to turn the tap on again. The problem was not thinking of the questions – I knew what I wanted to know about Daphne, every bit as much as I had known what I wanted to know about Elizabeth Barrett Browning or any other figure I've ever written about – but of realising that the answers would always depend on how the questions had been asked.

A journalist, of course, is used to this but I was not and the journalism involved in this kind of biography was far greater than I'd ever guessed. Any journalist knows that full frontal attacks are rarely productive – no good asking a son or daughter nasty questions about their parents' sex lives until you've known them a very long time. The trouble is, you never know what *they* know, or what they want you to know. A complicated game is played: prove you know something and I'll tell you about it.

Well, I'm not good at games but I had to learn this one quite quickly, and playing it always troubled me. Especially playing it with those who had been servants. I never lied, but I certainly indulged in a form of trickery. The trick was to pretend I knew something I only suspected – 'I'm told' I would say, and then come out with some inspired specu-lation. Faces would light up – oh, the relief people clearly felt that their lips were no longer sealed because someone else had blabbed first. Only once was I asked, in this kind of situation, who had told me and then I simply said I had sworn not to betray their confidence.

This, mind you, led on to another headache: what exactly is a confidence when you're researching someone's life? Biographies at the moment are full of those creatures I despise – those conveniently *un-named* 'friends' who say unspeakable and usually libellous things. I would never have any truck with 'em. But there is no doubt at all that, promised you will not divulge your source, people relax and speak more freely. So what to do? What I did was give, and keep, the promise. It meant never being able to quote some particularly interesting details but on the other hand it gave me access to an enormous amount of material which in the end helped me understand better. It was also a great benefit in another way: people learned to trust me and more than anything else I found trust was the key to so much – literally. After the first two years of building up trust it was astonishing how many drawers were unlocked, how many hitherto hidden letters presented to me.

But trust brought responsibility. All biographers ought to be responsible people whether their subjects have been dead two hundred or two years but the burden is far, far heavier the more recent the death. It is not so much the grave responsibility of trying to tell the truth – what is truth etc, we needn't get into that – but of deciding who knows the truth. Because everyone claims to. Try telling a distinguished octogenarian that their 'truth', of which they are utterly convinced and fiercely proud to know, is in direct contradiction to another's, equally in a position to know. It became not so much a matter of *what* do I believe as *whom* do I believe.

Back I would go to my first love, the written evidence. There were hundreds of letters to study and use when I was doing various nineteenth-century biographies, most of them printed and published, and I always felt happiest when doing that part of the work. But with Daphne du Maurier the letters became a kind of drug – I'd come back from some interviews feeling so confused and go to the letters and the confusion would clear. These were unpublished letters, written to a dozen or so close family and friends – quite separate from the scores of others written to a wider circle – and I relied on them heavily. Now, one school of thought thinks all letters are performances, and that therefore, especially where writers are concerned, they are highly suspect. I don't agree. A ten-year-old, writing to her governess who is on holiday, as Daphne wrote to hers, is not seeking to dissemble; a forty-year-old, writing to her dearest friend about the failure of her marriage, which she is desperately concealing from all around her, is not lying for effect. From letters like these Daphne's own judgment on whom to believe reassured me and guided me.

Nevertheless, there were secrets she didn't write about, secrets not about herself but about others. The things I know about her family and friends . . . things which have no place in her own biography. I felt, many times, like writing to her – a sort of 'Dear Daphne – My *god*, why didn't you tell me about what happened to X in 1959' letter. What did happen to X, and to Y and Z, was a whole other book, and I lived in terror in case X, Y and Z would discover I'd been told of their little dramas. I became the confidante of so many people and know I'm left the possessor of the most delicious but irrelevant (to this biography) stories. I am about to start a new novel. How a biographer goes straight from one life to another I do not know – I couldn't. It takes me a long, long time to stop thinking and talking about my last biography and the subjects of them never quite leave me. It is twenty years since I did Bonnie Prince Charlie and though, compared to Daphne du Maurier it is laughable to think I ever knew him at all, I still find myself suddenly remembering some tiny thing about him, for no reason at all. It is an exact definition to say of biography that it is obsessional. It is and because it is, it is dangerous. Everything, for a while, gets out of proportion and perspective is distorted. The relief of returning to fiction is immense: no worries, no responsibilities, just fun. I shall sleep sounder, and not be haunted by the fear of failure – failure to do justice to Daphne. With fiction, there is no fear. The only failure can be of intention and that matters only to me and not for long.

If ever I take on another biography – and in spite of all this gloomy talk of responsibility, I do love it – I think I would insist on being inspected by the family first (because, of course, now I've done an authorised biography and been first at the primary source material no other sort would tempt me except that of someone who had just died). I was lucky this time, terrifyingly lucky. The du Maurier estate appointed me without meeting me and I've never stopped thinking how dangerous that was, for all of us. Suppose I hadn't got on with Daphne's children and relations? Suppose they'd hated me? The book would have been a disaster. It is not that we needed to be chums but if we hadn't been able to communicate on quite a deep level, fifty per cent of the material would never have surfaced. And when things got tough, as they did, with dramatic and unexpected revelations at the last minute, this rapport was vital.

Well, no need for any rapport for the next year except with sheets of paper. But if writing novels is a doddle compared to writing biography, and if I'll be angst-free instead of bowed-down with worry, I'll miss one thing: the sense of satisfication in a difficult project completed. Biography is work, hard work, and fiction for me is lighthearted and fun. I enjoy the fun but I'll miss the work.

DOROTHY DUNNETT

Dorothy Dunnett was born in Dunfermline in 1923. She is known throughout the world for her historical novels which include the *Francis Crawford of Lymond* and the *House of Niccolò* series. She published her first novel in 1961 and to date has published twenty books. Dorothy Dunnett is also a professional portrait painter, and her interests include medieval history, archaeology, travel, sailing, opera and ballet. She lives in Edinburgh with her husband, Alastair.

WRITERS WRITING

Previous titles include:

The Game of Kings
Queens' Play
The Disorderly Knight
Pawn in Frankincense
The Ringed Castle
Checkmate
King Hereafter

Niccolò Rising
The Spring of the Ram
Race of Scorpions
Scales of Gold
the *Johnson Johnson* series
The Scottish Highlands

DOROTHY DUNNETT

The Comfort of Dreams

To write any novel requires a suspension of lethargy. To choose to write serial novels set in an early historical period is to become a hermit, supported by a circle of frayed-looking librarians and a travel agent with spunk ('Mrs Dunnett, how do we book you into a monastery?').

The first novel in a historical series is a cinch – a straightforward slog through large quantities of popular source material, and a less straightforward slog, depending on conscience, through a smaller, stickier quantity of primary sources. Military and political facts are not hard to come by, if you don't mind five different versions of each event. It is much harder to find out whether, for example, people blew their noses modestly (no) and what they slept in (a hat).

Facts in hand, the romancer then proceeds to the addictive pleasure of slotting in the required fiction to proportion (the infinite variety of proportion is what gives historical fiction its appeal and slightly drunken charm). The problem of period language is irrevocably settled, one way or another, in this first book. A number of other matters are also irrevocably settled, some of them by default, unless you take heed. Planning a series is like planning a war.

By the third or fourth book, the researching writer has made a discovery. Common facts are quickly exhausted, and the business of acquiring uncommon facts is expensive, time-consuming and formidably attractive. Alienation from friends and family now begins, as original maps and esoteric books in unusual languages are loaded on to aircraft, and travel luggage acquires larger wheels. As the boundaries of published material fall behind, the romancer is left in a rosy, nebulous landscape containing the alluring highway of original research.

This is even more expensive, even more time-consuming and probably wholly unwise. The compulsion to embark on it, apart from natural nosiness, derives from the remembered delight of discovering that the facts and the background of a loved book were authentic, and might be pursued, and seized, and assimilated. From such enthusiasms are true historians (they tell me) sometimes made. The compulsion to compose novels from such material is something else, and indicates a severe character defect on the part of the author.

It is shared by others. The building I write in is wryly code-named by my household 'the dream factory', because that's what it is. It's a recognition of the fact that a large portion of the human race requires the comfort of dreams; requires rest from reality; requires a role model, it might be. Some of that, people draw from other arts, and other forms of the novel. The special attraction of the historical novel seems to lie in its remoteness from the present day: escape from reality is immediate. At its most compelling the historical novel can have a range of emotional impact somewhat equivalent to both the binge and the fix.

It has also, I suppose, one particular asset. It can be read (and written) in maturity as well as immaturity; because of its nature it presents facets which reflect many different aspects of the human condition, and which can open different doors to different ages. Or is that unduly pretentious? (Yes.) Perhaps what we all really like, and keep dog-eared on our bookshelves are the flamboyant, heroic, outrageous historical novels of our youth, with all their excesses and errors and glorious confidence. In which case, roll on the next generation of historical writers.

P. D. JAMES

(Photo: Nigel Parry)

P. D. James was born in Oxford in 1920 and educated at Cambridge High School. From 1949 to 1968 she worked in the National Health Service as an administrator, and the experiences gained there helped with creating the background for a number of her novels. In 1968 she joined the Home Office as Principal, working first in the Police Department concerned with the forensic science service, and later in the Criminal Policy Department. She retired in 1979 and is currently a Fellow of the Royal Society of Literature, a Fellow of the Royal Society of Arts, a Governor of the BBC and a member of the Board of the British Council. She was until the summer of 1992 a member of the Board of the Arts Council and Chairman of its Literature Advisory Panel. She is a member of the Management Committee of the Royal Society of Literature.

P. D. James has twice been the winner of the Silver Dagger Award of the Crime Writers' Association, and in 1987 she was awarded the Diamond Dagger Award for services to crime writing. In 1983 she received the OBE and in 1991 was created a life peer as Baroness James of Holland Park.

Previous titles include:

Cover Her Face
A Mind to Murder
Unnatural Causes
Shroud for a Nightingale
An Unsuitable Job for a Woman
The Black Tower

Death of an Expert Witness
Innocent Blood
The Skull Beneath the Skin
A Taste for Death
Devices and Desires
The Children of Men

RUTH RENDELL

(Photo: Sally Soames)

Ruth Rendell was born in South Woodford, London. After attending school in Loughton, she became a journalist on local newspapers, and edited the *Chigwell Times*. She is married to Don Rendell, who was also a journalist, and they have one son. She began her writing career by producing at least six novels, none of which she tried to publish. She did offer some short stories, all of which were rejected. She is a prolific writer and as well as her novels, she has published volumes of short stories and a book on Suffolk, her current home. Her husband is always her first reader and critic. They live in a large country house, with a number of cats, and also in London.

Ruth Rendell is a Fellow of the Royal Society of Literature and has an Honorary Doctorate from the University of Essex.

Previous titles include:

An Unkindness of Ravens
The Best Man to Die
The Veiled One
Going Wrong

The Copper Peacock
Murder Being Once Done
*Kissing the Gunner's
  Daughter*

RUTH RENDELL and P. D. JAMES

Series Detectives

P. D. JAMES We are both described as crime writers, but what does that actually mean? There's an extraordinary variety of crime writing; on one hand you have the cosy certainties of Dame Agatha and Mahem Parva, and on the other such writers as Dickens, Wilkie Collins, Graham Greene, the great Russian novelists and some of the highest works of the human imagination. They could all be termed crime novelists; there is an extraordinary variety.

I write the classical detective story and it does have a kind of formula. What you expect is a mysterious death, a closed circle of suspects, a detective, either amateur or professional, and by the end a solution which the reader should be able to arrive at by logical deduction from the clues inserted in the book with essential fairness but deceptive cunning. I would, however, deny that this is merely formula writing. You, Ruth, both write within the classical formula and outside it. To me your most interesting works are the Barbara Vine books, superb novels by any standard. The Wexford books, however, are within the tradition.

RUTH RENDELL I do think that Wexford is a 'fantasic' figure whereas Dalgliesh is a real policeman. Any small Suffolk town that had quite as many murders as Kingsmarkham would be rivalling the worst areas in

New York City for daily death, and of course we know that doesn't happen.

P. D. JAMES Was it Chandler who said he wanted to write realistic books? He very much disliked the English murder story, in fact he despised it. He said that the English were not necessarily the best writers in the world but they were the best dull writers, and he was thinking of detective novels. But, of course, a Chandler book is complete fantasy. He has his hero striding down the mean streets like a kind of modern knight in white armour – he's just as much a figure of fantasy as people might argue Dalgliesh and Wexford are. A novel is an artificial form, and none the worst for that. It's a matter of selection.

RUTH RENDELL I think you've got to have a measure of reality in crime fiction, especially when a police investigation is happening. You have got to have things that really could happen and not juggle about with clocks and time and trains.

P. D. JAMES You've got to have a realistic story, not one which depends on the murderer having an alibi which meant he caught a train at two minutes to the hour in time to catch a bus. Well, that wouldn't work today. We know that the train would have been cancelled and the bus would be late!

Nowadays readers are much more sophisticated and knowledgeable about police procedure and we have to try to get it right. In those wonderful days of Agatha Christie there was no distinction between the CID and the ordinary police. The dear old bobby cycled off to the scene of the crime and the post mortem was done by the village GP after his surgery – and on the same table, presumably. The next morning he would tell the talented detective more about how the victim died than a modern forensic laboratory could tell you in a fortnight!

We've come a long way from that, and one of the most difficult problems is that most police work is a matter of rather dull administrative routine. In novels we want our hero to solve the crime single-handedly. In real life that would never happen.

RUTH RENDELL I can remember when I was a child, no longer reading children's books, wondering why nobody wrote about the sort of background I lived in. Why did nobody write about the middle class, about people who lived in suburban houses with three bedrooms and a bathroom and a third of an acre of garden like me? Nobody ever did and this applied right through literature. I don't think it was confined to crime fiction. What has happened [in more recent times] has been a social change, not a literary change.

I always say that I came into crime writing by accident, but I don't think this is absolutely true. The first book of mine to be published happened to be a crime novel – the first *Wexford* – but I had written other fiction which might equally have been published had I persisted. But I think I must have had a natural bent that way because I always wanted, whatever kind of fiction I wrote, to make it exciting. Even now I can't write anything that hasn't got a lot of plot. I need the novel of mood and atmosphere.

P. D. JAMES I absolutely agree with you: there should be action and excitement. There is this distinction between the novels which people really want to read and those which are highly regarded which you read as a kind of chore. Every now and then I say to myself, for God's sake, you're seventy-one, life's too short.

I deliberately started with detective stories because I very much enjoyed reading them, and Dorothy L. Sayers was a strong influence on my childhood. I thought if I was able to construct a detective story it would stand a good chance of being accepted because it was a popular form. I love construction in a novel and I like strong narrative drive. In setting out as a detective writer I wasn't expecting to make a lot of money but I did have a high ambition to be regarded as a serious novelist. I thought that writing a detective story would be a wonderful apprenticeship because, whatever people tell you, a crime novel is not easy to write well. As I continued with my craft I became increasingly fascinated by the form and realised that you can use the formula to say something true about men and women and the society in which they live. I think that is what Ruth and I are trying to do; writing good novels in a form which intrigues and interests us.

RUTH RENDELL I didn't originally conceive of Wexford as part of a series – if I had I would have made him a lot younger for one thing – by about thirty-five years! I called him Reg because my favourite uncle was called Reg. I think he may be partly based on my father, but quite a lot of him is me. He started off as a rather tough cop but when I realised I was stuck with him as a series character, I began to make him more literate and sensitive and more interesting, I hope. At one point I thought I'd made him a bit too soft and toughened him up! I think readers love series fiction. Phyllis [P. D. James] has more than one series character whereas I have only one, and I've written fifteen [now sixteen] books about him and a number of short stories. I feel I have exhausted his potential, and that I'm tired of him. It's not that I have exhausted the possibilities of exploring his character but I have exhausted the possibilities of things he can do in his limited environment. I don't think that I am going to get involved with the local constabulary. I could do that, but I don't really think I will because there are a lot of other things I want to do.

I don't want to begin again with any other series character but as for series writing in general, I enjoy writing about an ongoing character.

P. D. JAMES When I began, I made conscious choices. I don't think that I really expected Dalgliesh would go on to feature in a series of books but I thought I'd better begin with a detective who could.

First of all I had to decide whether I was going to have an amateur or a professional. There are a lot of advantages in a way in having an amateur because you can have a detective of either sex, any age. You can give him or her an interesting private life, you can send them all over the country and you can give them a hobby that happens to be your hobby. There aren't all the constraints of Force procedure and judges' rules. But, of course, on the other hand, a certain amount of credibility does go out of the window. Ruth was saying that with Wexford, the local murder rate is somewhat above the average. Indeed, when you think of amateur detectives or whatever stumbling over bodies, it really is quite extraordinary! I've never found a corpse, I hope I never will. If you do find a corpse, there are two things that you can do. One is to walk on and pretend you haven't seen it, and the other is to phone the police. You don't want to investigate it, do you?

There are certain advantages in writing about your series character because you have created him and you know absolutely everything about him so that when you begin your new book, your central character, who in a sense holds the book together, is already caught. You know him, you approve of him because if you didn't you wouldn't want to go on writing about him, and your readers wouldn't like him. It is a strong incentive to go on but I agree – you can get to a point (I'm not at it yet) when you feel that he has been exhausted. If that point comes, I'm sure that I could not kill him off. I thought the other day that I would kill him off and I was amazed how horrified I was at the idea of doing it. I realised that psychologically it was a kind of suicide.

RUTH RENDELL There is a rather new school of women crime writers with female private eyes who in some ways are just as tough as their male counterparts. I think, personally, that's a rather American development. I think they have more sensitivity and I think they are more human despite the fact that you know they're pretty tough characters. I prefer them to the males, I must say, they are more interesting. But I don't think I would be able to write about that type of woman, really, or particularly want to.

P. D. JAMES No, I wouldn't want to. I think also that quite a lot of interest is simply because they are women. It's still a matter of being surprised that women do this at all. I don't find this very believable and that's the stumbling block for me.

RUTH RENDELL A policeman once told me that no DI could remain so prudish and Victorian as Burden, who has been described as the most miserable detective in fiction. I disagreed with that then, and I disagree with that now. But anyway, I thought that I had better do something about him. So I killed his wife and let him have this very torrid affair. I thought that would sort of change him a bit, but, in spite of me, he went back to what he was!

P. D. JAMES It might be that the police don't read much detective fiction. I do get a great deal of help from Scotland Yard and the head of the Murder Squad did once say of Dalgliesh, 'he's a good cop', which struck me as high praise. I don't expect them to take a strong interest, I must say, but they are very kind and they will always help with advice.

I have always been interested in the reason why detective fiction in particular is so popular and, of course, there are obvious reasons which we touched on earlier. You do get a story, you get a beginning, a middle and an end. You get excitement. Murder is a unique crime for which we can never make reparation. We are living in an age when any of us might meet our end by any terrorist in any airport lounge. I think basically that we want to believe that we live in a morally comprehensible universe and that we are able to solve problems, again in an age when many problems are really beyond the capacity of man's intellect to solve. To do so is comforting and bears on that central problem of our mortality. Maybe it's saying that even death itself is only really a puzzle which in the end we will be able to solve. I'm told that most people do not think about death at all and pretend it's not going to happen – we live in an age where there is a prevailing view that you can somehow avoid it altogether.

RUTH RENDELL We might argue that modern detective fiction brings real death before you so that you get used to it. If I am ignorant and want some reassurance, I am probably going to pick up an Agatha Christie or a Dorothy L. Sayers, because it is not really dealing with reality. It is not threatening and therefore it has a comforting result. This is nothing to be ashamed of. We need it and we are entitled to take comfort. It does seem to me to be one reason why this form has been so popular. It is distancing the fear and it enables you to deal with your own guilt. When Wexford or Dalgliesh or Miss Marple or Poirot or Lord Peter points the accusing finger, we are able to say a confident 'not guilty'.

[When researching] I don't keep any notes at all except when I am actually writing a book and when I have a few things that I ought to remember.

P. D. JAMES I am afraid I am a great keeper of notebooks. I don't go anywhere without a notebook and I think I had about fourteen for *Devices and Desires*. But that does not prevent me from making the odd careless mistake.

RUTH RENDELL We all make them, of course, and we see them very triumphantly in the work of others! I must say that I haven't seen any in Phyllis's.

P. D. JAMES I think everyone's heard about the motorbike. Haven't you?

RUTH RENDELL Only because you told me!

P. D. JAMES I think it was in my second book when I had a suspect wearing goggles and leathers on a motorbike and I wrote than he reversed noisily down the lane. Then I had a letter (and it would be from a man reader), which said, 'Dear Mrs James, you are usually so meticulous in your use of language, but I was surprised to find you used the word "reverse" which almost gives the impression that you think a two-stroke motor-cycle engine can go backwards.' Well, of course, I did think it could! It was a very silly mistake and I still get letters from all over the world from gentlemen, explaining to me in tedious technical detail (often with a diagram), precisely why a two-stroke engine can't.

Then, about six months ago, I got a postcard which simply said, 'It can if it's a Harley Davidson.' So if anyone else raises the point of the motorbike, I say, 'It's a Harley Davidson!'

From a 'Meet the Author' event at the 1991 Festival.

Inspirations

THE CREATIVE PROCESS.

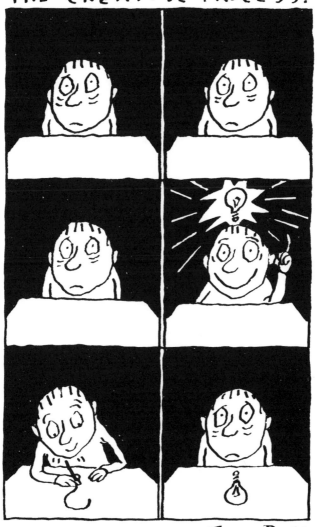

Illustration by Tony Ross

Tony Ross

ANGELA LAMBERT

(Photo: Nicholas Cook)

Angela Lambert was born in Kent but spent most of her childhood in Germany and Finland. She was sent to a girls' boarding school for seven years – an experience exorcised thirty years later by writing *No Talking After Lights*. She read PPE at St Hilda's College, Oxford, and was a television reporter for sixteen years, first on *News at Ten* and then with London Weekend and Thames Television.

She is currently a feature writer and columnist for the *Independent* and a member of the executive committee of English PEN. Her first book, *Unquiet Souls*, was runner-up for the Whitbread Prize for Biography in 1984. She is currently at work on her fourth novel, *Laura's Dozen*, and recently had the flash-point for her fifth! She lives in London with her partner. When possible, she goes to France to write.

Previous titles include:

Unquiet Souls
Love Among the Single Classes
No Talking After Lights
A Rather English Marriage

ANGELA LAMBERT

Lowering the Bucket, or How I Write

There is a moment that occurs once, at most twice, a year and is exactly like the moment at which you know you're going to catch a cold. But instead of that sharp treacherous tickle at the back of the nose which heralds days of heavy-headedness (and – forgive this motherly footnote – can often be averted by taking a huge dose of Vitamin C immediately) in *this* case, I know I've caught a book.

An idea seizes me with its intensity, dazzles like a brilliant flame at the end of a long dark tunnel of imagination, and there, I *know*, is the next book. In the case of my first novel, the idea came in the form of a dream so vivid that when I woke up, I rushed to write it down in half a dozen sentences. Since I had just embarked – I thought – on a career as a non-fiction writer, I was nonplussed by this inconvenient but detailed plot, and not sure what to do with it. I decided to sit down each evening for a week and write until I stopped (half an hour? an hour? two? I wasn't sure) without looking back at what I had written the previous day. At the end of the week I would read what I had written and see what it amounted to. The answer was, seven thousand words and the opening chapter of *Love Among the Single Classes*. (By way of another footnote, I lost the notebook in which I had jotted down the original plot and didn't rediscover it for eighteen months, by which time the novel had been published. I was astonished to see how faithfully my eventual book had followed that first flash of an idea.)

No other book has been quite as easy to spark off or to write as that. I dreamed it in a flash and wrote it in five months. When it came to the second novel, I knew only that I wanted it to be entirely different: I was determined not to turn out a production line of poignant stories of lost love. (Though it would have been quite easy, and they seem to sell rather well.)

Having wasted a good deal of time trying to convince readers that the first novel was not autobiographical, I decided the second one might as well be. I was sent to boarding school at the age of ten, more than forty years ago, having been given no choice in the matter. I stayed there, furiously unhappy, until I was seventeen. When I left, I determined to put the whole episode behind me; never to revisit my old school and not if possible to think about it. Within a year or two I had even ceased to keep in touch with my school friends. Apart from the occasional insistent nightmare, my seven years in the heart of Sussex were buried deep and undisturbed. It then occurred to me that I had here perfect fictional material: and that was the genesis of *No Talking After Lights*.

It began, unlike the first novel, with no plot and hardly any characters, just the setting: the absolutely vivid and (as it transpired) totally recalled classrooms, buildings, gardens, tennis courts and games field of my old school. I did not, until the book was almost finished, revisit it to verify my recollections. Instead, I lowered the bucket of memory into the deep well of the unconscious mind, and gazed in amazement at the wriggling words ('Hard cheese!', 'Stale buns and bad bananas!', 'So squish to you too!') and painful images (tears; fibs; letters from home; being sent to Coventry and given an apple-pie bed; more tears) that it came up with.

That book was more difficult to write, and took longer than the first. But over the course of eighteen months or so, I came to trust the absolute accuracy of these old memories, which I now know lie hidden in the unconscious mind waiting to be called upon. The difficulty came in finding a *plot*, and furthermore, the plot of an adult novel rather than a teenage boarding-school story. I managed it in the end, but only thanks to much help and prompting from my partner and my editor at Hamish Hamilton.

When I started to think about the third novel, the flashpoint was different again, but equally precise. Lunching in France one Sunday in April, I noticed two elderly Englishmen at the next table. They were evidently not related (one asked about the other's sister) and they seemed not to be gay. Yet they lived together, that was clear from the proprietary way in which they both addressed the dog that lay quietly under their table. What, I wondered, idly, brings two men, not related, not lovers, to share a home? And how does it work? That speculation was the starting point for *A Rather English Marriage*.

Once the book was underway it became a sort of technical puzzle I set myself – to examine marriage through the eyes of two men – and one made more difficult by the fact that their wives die in the opening pages. I had to find a convincing language through which the reader would learn about the married lives of these two widowers, but without ever meeting or hearing directly from their wives. I had to find a voice for two people of the opposite gender from myself, made harder still by the fact that they were twenty years older than I am.

The clue turned out to lie in the plot – and a rollicking plot it proved to be when I got into my stride! – and, once again, *memory*. I lowered the bucket into the deep well of the unconscious again, and set myself to remember the lost details of my parents and their friends in the 1940s and '50s. How had they talked? How had they behaved towards one another? What were the manners of men to their wives; what the demeanour of wives to husbands then? It all came flooding back: from the bird's-eye view of my eight-year-old self as ball boy (never ball girl) at their summer tennis doubles, or through the ears of the ten-year-old me, ignored and supposedly reading in a corner of the room. The very tone and timbre of their conversations returned, down to the tiniest detail.

I learned, through my second and third novels, to put my trust in the wealth and veracity of memory. I am sure it is all there and just as complete for everyone, but only writers and the old put such faith in it. Someone – Balzac, was it? – said 'Imagination is memory'. I have found that view to be absolutely right.

BRIAN MOORE

Brian Moore was born in 1921 in Belfast and was educated there at St Malachy's College. He served with the British Ministry of War Transport during the latter part of the Second World War in North Africa, Italy and France. After the war, he worked for the United Nations in Europe before emigrating to Canada in 1948, where he became a journalist and adopted Canadian citizenship. He spent some time in New York and then moved to California, where he now lives and works.

(Photo: Julian Lee)

Five of his novels have been made into films. He has twice won the Canadian Governor General's Award for Fiction and has been given a special award from the United States Institute of Arts and Letters. He has won the Authors' Club First Novel Award, the WH Smith Literary Award and the James Tait Black Memorial Prize. Brian Moore has also been shortlisted for the Booker Prize three times, in 1976, 1987 and 1990. In 1988, *The Colour of Blood* was named the *Sunday Express* Book of the Year. *Lies of Silence* is his best-selling novel to date.

WRITERS WRITING

Previous titles include:

The Doctor's Wife   *The Luck of Ginger Coffey*
Black Robe   *The Colour of Blood*
The Emperor of Ice-Cream   *Lies of Silence*
The Lonely Passion of Judith Hearne   *No Other Life*

BRIAN MOORE

Imagination and Experience

This is from Henri Troyat's biography of Leo Tolstoy which deals with the period in Tolstoy's life when he had begun to write *Anna Karenina*. He laboured away at the manuscript full of distrust, anger and weariness. He made revision after revision, and felt that he was taking two steps backward for one step forward.

> There are days when one gets up feeling clear-headed and refreshed. One begins to write, everything is fine, it all comes naturally. The next day one reads it over and it all has to go because the heart isn't there, no imagination, no talent, that *quelque chose* is lacking without which our intelligence is worthless. Other days one gets up hating the world, nerves completely on edge; nevertheless one hopes to get something done. And indeed it doesn't go too badly. It's fitted, there's imagination by the carload. Again one reads it over. Meaning-less, stupid, the brain wasn't there. Imagination and intelli-gence have to work together. As soon as one gets the upper hand all is lost. There is nothing to be done but throw away what you have done and start over.

Anyone who is a novelist knows that paragraph accurately describes the period in writing a novel when the characters and scenes refuse to move forward and the writer is in

197

danger of suffering that accidie in which novels die. The elements Tolstoy is trying to put in balance are what he calls imagination and intelligence. Imagination we understand but what is this intelligence he speaks of? Is it the intelligence of the novelist who has written other novels and knows he is following the tightrope which he must walk in order to keep the story alive and suspend the reader's disbelief? I think it is, but it's also something else. It's the faculty of balancing the fiction one is writing against the facts of one's life and the lives of people one knows, a faculty which Hemingway accurately but inelegantly called a built-in bullshit detector.

And so we come back to the question of experience – the hand which real life has dealt us and which some of us attempt to play out in our novels. Unfortunately for most of us there are not enough cards to sustain us. Unlike Tolstoy, most of us do not lead interesting lives. And if, like me, you have been solely a novelist for many years, you have long ago ceased to live anything like a normal existence – you have no regular job, you spend most of your days alone in a room, you do not have a communal workplace which allows you to observe the behaviour of others. If you have friends they tend to be other writers, academics, actors: people who, as Flaubert pointed out, are not living lives that correspond to the lives of most of your readers. Your invented characters assume an ever increasing importance in your life. If what Tolstoy called intelligence means experience of real life, you are no longer a frontline witness. I think this feeling of isolation and distance from real life is the reason so many people write one or two novels then stop and become teachers, dramatists or pundits. And the problem is exacerbated by the fact we no longer live in a cohesive society as the great nineteenth-century novelists did. We cannot assume that our readers will confidently follow us into the worlds we write about, as did the readers of Balzac and Dickens. It becomes increasingly difficult to create a realistic novelistic universe.

Let's return to Tolstoy who, unlike most novelists, lived a full life. He was an aristocrat who fought bravely in military campaigns. In his youth he was a gambler, a womaniser, a heavy drinker, irresponsible and often dissolute. But he also had the soul of a saint, a flawed saint who railed against injustice. Yet in the most interesting and creative period of his life he did not use his past experience accurately in his novels. That novel *Anna Karenina*, which was giving him so much trouble, was set in motion by his chancing to hear of the mistress of a neighbour who had thrown herself under a train because her lover was planning to jilt her. The following day Tolstoy went to the station where the autopsy was being performed. Staring at the ugly, mutilated body he tried to imagine the existence of this woman who had senselessly died for love. Imagination. A chance remark, a newspaper clipping, an overheard story: how often are these slight-seeming things the genesis for a novel. But almost always it seems that this synthesis occurs because these things connect with a novelist's preoccupations or obsessions. Infidelity and violent death had been in Tolstoy's mind for some time. A few years earlier he had told his wife that he wanted to write about an upper-class woman guilty of adultery. That morning in the railway station looking at the dead body of a discarded mistress, not upper-class, not guilty of adultery, the magical moment occurred. Imagination and intelligence suddenly came together. The hard work in writing the novel lay ahead, but the obsession had taken hold of him and would not leave him. Imagination and intelligence did not desert him. The result was a masterpiece.

And it is imagination, the ability to become characters very different from oneself, which differentiates him from lesser writers. He started by writing about 'a woman who was pitiable but not contemptible', but as he continued to write and as he made the imaginative step into the character's mind, he actually fell in love with Anna. It is this quality of empathy which makes it one of the great novels. And this is what I find fascinating. Fifteen years later the novel was long dead in his mind. When praised for this work he seemed to regret having written it and dismissed it as a tawdry tale of adultery. He had forgotten his love affair with Anna.

In that final rejection and misunderstanding of his work Tolstoy proved himself to be a true novelist. For when a novel is finished the true novelist begins to forget what he has written. When the act of writing is over, imagination and intelligence desert him, and his opinions on the merits of his book have no more weight than the opinions of anyone else.

If you believe that statement – and I do – there is nothing intelligent I can say about my own work. But perhaps I can discuss briefly something which I have experienced: the life of a novelist self-exiled from his own country who discovered after he had written three novels set from his own birthplace that he could no longer comfortably go out in that past. When I wrote my first novel I was twenty-six years old and had emigrated to Canada. I had spent some years in Italy, France and Poland, yet it did not occur to me to write about those places. My literary hero at the time was James Joyce, who had managed to write his entire *oeuvre* about Dublin which he had abandoned in his twenties to live permanently in Europe. When I started to write I too wrote about the place of my birth, but my birthplace was Belfast and, unlike Joyce, I remembered my native city with a mixture of anger and bitterness which made me want to write it out of my system and look for a new world in which I and my characters could live. From then on from time to time Ireland would appear in my novels, but it was not until 1989 that I returned to Belfast as a setting for one of my books. In my third novel, *The Luck of Ginger Coffey*, my character and I emigrated to Canada. And later my novels followed the course of my emigration moving on with me to New York and California.

By the time I had written my fourth novel, which was set in New York, I knew that my books could no longer follow the rather mundane events of my existence. From that time on each novel was for me a new beginning; I was forced to rely on imagination and experimentation. Luckily I had begun to read Borges, a writer whose work was very different from my own. I saw how he created imaginary worlds which seemed totally real and how the fantastic could seem mundane, simply through the great skill of writing. And so I abandoned the realism of my early novels and since then have written in several styles and used many different locations. I've gone back into the past to write about a Jesuit priest in the seventeenth century who goes on a dangerous journey into the Canadian wilderness. About a cardinal in Eastern Europe on the run from his political enemies. I've

written about a man's dream of visualising a collection of
Victoriana in a parking lot in Carmel, California, and what
happened when he awoke from that dream and finds the
collection had materialised exactly as he had dreamt it. I've
written about a beautiful young woman of no religious
beliefs who, in the middle of an adulterous affair, believes
she sees an apparition of the Virgin Mary, and what happens
to her when she chooses to ignore that vision.

Each of these novels has been a new beginning and in the
course of writing I have used forms which would not have
occurred to me in the days when my masters were Joyce and
Flaubert. I've written an adventure tale in a Conradian
manner, metaphysical thrillers, allegorical fantasies and
novels in which the natural and supernatural co-exist in
dangerous proximity. What I'm trying to say is that my life in
exile has forced me to become a literary chameleon. I
sometimes wonder what would have happened to me had I
not left Ireland and continued to write novels based on the
world into which I was born. For me, fiction is not the story
of my life or the lives of people I have known. It's a struggle
to write novels which will in some way reflect my own
experience through the adventures of my characters. Novels
permit me to re-examine beliefs I no longer hold, and search
for some meaning in my life. The writing of novels has
become my *raison d'être*.

As a last comment on the question of imagination and
experience I would like to quote from the German poet
Novalis who wrote that genius is the capacity to deal with
imagined objects as with real ones and to accord them the
same kind of treatment. It differs from the talent to present
something, to observe them exactly and to give a fitting
account of the thing observed. We are not geniuses, most of
us who write, but we are many of us people who have chosen
the surrogate life of the imagination. We have perhaps
settled for that state which Wallace Stevens speaks of, 'the
final belief is to believe in a fiction which you know to be a
fiction, there being nothing else'.

From a paper commissioned for the International Writers Conference
at the 1991 Festival

PENELOPE LIVELY

(Photo: Jerry Bauer)

Penelope Lively grew up in Egypt but settled in England after the war and took a degree in history at St Anne's College, Oxford. She has been shortlisted for the Booker Prize three times, winning it in 1987 with *Moon Tiger*. She has also won the Southern Arts Literature Award and the first National Book Award and has been shortlisted for the Whitbread Award and the *Sunday Express* Book of the Year Award. Her short stories have appeared in magazines, including foreign periodicals. Her work has been widely translated and a number of short stories and novels have been read on BBC and Australian radio. She has written radio and television scripts and presented the BBC Radio 4 programme on children's literature, *Treasure Islands*. She is a popular writer for children and has been awarded the Carnegie Medal.

Penelope Lively is a fellow of the Royal Society of Literature and a member of PEN and the Society of Authors. She is married to Professor Jack Lively, has a daughter, a son, two granddaughters and a grandson, and lives in Oxfordshire and London.

Previous titles include:

The Road to Lichfield
Nothing Missing but the
  Samovar
Treasures of Time
Judgement Day
According to Mark

Pack of Cards
Moon Tiger
Passing On
City of the Mind
Cleopatra's Sister

PENELOPE LIVELY

An Airy Communion with a Notebook

I sometimes think that the most exhilarating time in the writing of a book is before it is ever begun. The arrival of the idea, which stalks up furtively when least expected. The gestation – when you never seem to be actively thinking about it but somehow it is quietly firming up. And then, usually for me, the slow and enjoyable process of not writing the book but reading about it. Discovering its background, furnishing it with a landscape and a climate.

I refuse to apply the word research to this activity. It has connotations of scholarship which are inappropriate. A novelist is not a scholar, nor should be – the accuracies that are being sought are of a different order. They are indeed accuracies – if I am writing about war-time London then I must get things right. What happened when, and where. And if my central character is a palaeontologist then I must know what it is he is doing, and what his career structure might be, and what his problems and preoccupations are likely to be. But the reading has got to be random as well as investigative. I have got to read in all directions, because at this stage I do not know exactly what it is that I need to know, and what I learn is going to determine what I write. I must read far more than I will ever need to have read. Most of the reading is simply ballast – none of it will ever show, but it must be there for the sake of stability. It is that hidden

WRITERS WRITING

substance from which the entire book has sprung. Not every novel requires all this. Several have needed none at all. Then, the gestation process is simply an airy communion with a notebook which gradually fills with snatches of dialogue, descriptions, experimental scenes – some of which will end up in the finished product and some of which will not. But others cannot begin until I have spent weeks and months reading and jotting down this and that and recognising that eventually the point will come when I know that enough is enough, the foundations have been laid, and I can get out the notebook and begin.

The British Library is my saviour at these times. I love it. I love the heady feeling that you can summon up absolutely anything. I love browsing through the catalogue and discovering the things I never knew I needed to read, and hitting accidentally upon the book which precisely meshes with my current preoccupation. I spend whole days in there, with a packet of Marks & Spencer sandwiches in my bag so that when I need a break I can go and sit in the courtyard with the droves of schoolchildren and the pigeons.

This reading is in some ways random but it is also deliberate. I know at this point what this book is going to be about, and therefore what it is that I am looking for. I know that it is a book about the way in which a city is a reflection of all those who look at it, and that I am setting it in London and that therefore there are particular aspects of London's history and topography about which I need to know. Or I have become fired with an idea about the nature of choice and contingency, and I want to invent a non-existent North African country, and in order to do that I must read a great deal of Mediterranean history in order to make my country plausible. But before that there will have been the moment when the lightning struck, when all of a sudden I knew where the next novel was coming from and that moment cannot be hunted down in the British Library, or anywhere else. It either comes, or it doesn't.

But in my case it comes, more often than not, from something that I have been reading. Books beget books. At any one time I am likely to be reading several books – some intently, some in a desultory way. It is a sort of compulsive

206

foraging, I realise – based on the instinct that that is from whence my own next inspiration will arrive. Actually, I dislike the term inspiration also. I never feel inspired, merely fired. And the fire is fuelled by reading. There is an obsession – about the operation of memory, or the nature of evidence, or the process of contingency – and the obsession prompts a certain direction of reading, or else means that in some eerie way almost everything read is understood in a light pertinent to the obsession. There is a marvellous process, I have discovered, whereby when you are generating a book, everything that happens becomes mysteriously relevant to that book. You read something that is exactly what you need, someone makes the perfectly apposite remark, you stumble across the street scene or the social exchange which is entirely apt.

There is no point in going out in search of a novel, I have learned. At the moment, I have very little idea what my next novel will be about, or even if there will be one. But if there is, it will come creeping up on me, first as the flicker of an idea, then as a sort of fictional climate, and eventually as a story kitted out with characters and a setting. But if I sat down on Monday morning with the intention of working out a theme and a structure for the book, then nothing would happen at all. The only way in which I can help the process along is by pretending to be unconcerned. And the pretence of unconcern means just getting on with day-to-day life, which certainly includes as much reading as possible, and as much random and disordered reading as possible. My idea of a few days ostensibly doing nothing would include a great deal of browsing along bookshelves – libraries, bookshops, my own – and dipping in and out of books for no particular reason except that my hand happened to light on that one. And, like as not, something will feed a current preoccupation, and that in turn will eventually be reincarnated as a full-blown fictional idea.

And after that it is merely a question of finding the story and the characters and the setting. Merely . . . A process which can take up to a year or so before the writing begins. But by then there is a certain inevitability. Once the idea arrives, then it seems in some uncanny way to bring with it hints and suggestions about the presentation. The characters lurk in its wake; it already proposes a landscape and a language. I know that there is a long haul ahead, and that at points I shall get disillusioned, or lose confidence, or simply fail to see where to go next. But the book will get written. The most precarious, and in some ways the most exciting part of the sequence is always that fallow period right at the start. Waiting. Reading.

JOHN MORTIMER

(Photo: Sally Soames)

John Mortimer is a playwright, novelist and former practising barrister. During the war, he worked with the Crown Film Unit and published a number of novels before turning to the theatre with such plays as *The Dock Brief*, *The Wrong Side of the Park* and *A Voyage Round My Father*. He has written many film scripts, radio and television plays including six plays on the life of Shakespeare, the *Rumpole* plays, which won him the British Academy Writer of the Year Award, and the adaptation of Evelyn Waugh's *Brideshead Revisited*. His translations of Feydeau have been performed at the National Theatre. His novels *Paradise Postponed* and *Summer's Lease* were made into successful television series. He lives with his wife and their two daughters in what was once his father's house in the Chilterns.

Previous titles include:

the *Rumpole* series
Clinging to the Wreckage
A Voyage Round My Father
Charade
Like Men Betrayed
The Narrowing Stream

Paradise Postponed
Summer's Lease
Dunster
Titmuss Regained
The Rapstone Chronicles

JOHN MORTIMER

A Plot at Last

Asked what he would like to have written on his tombstone a working novelist said, 'A plot at last.'

The never-ending struggle for a story is the hardest, and least controllable, task a writer faces. The construction of sentences, prose rhythms and the flow of dialogue, all these, like an ear for music or a knack for doing quadratic equations, are attributes you have to be born with. Themes occur to philosophers and journalists as well as to novelists. Descriptive writing means looking about you clearly. Characters come from perpetual curiosity about people's private lives and taking the trouble to remember their bizarre ways with the language. But plots come from – God knows where. They can't be summoned at will. They arrive reluctantly, unexpectedly, stealthily, when you have given up all hope of them ever paying you a visit. Dickens described the desperate search for stories, the constant getting up from the desk, going to the window, sitting down hopelessly, the twenty-mile walks across the countryside or through the dark and deserted streets of London. He needed plots more than food, money, richly embroidered waistcoats or the company of young actresses. And then, at a blessed moment after so much grief and pain, he would scribble a few notes on a scrap of paper and he had got it. A plot at last!

Is all this agony necessary? Is a story an old-fashioned contrivance which has, like fountain-pens and blotting paper, gone out of style in an age of word processors? Many highly thought of, prize-winning novels do without stories and rely on atmosphere and semi-poetic writing. Well, Dickens was the master of strange atmosphere, his writing was frequently poetic, not to say theatrical, and yet he managed a story as well. Perhaps it's the absence of plots which has caused an unfortunate split in modern novel-writing; because the audience dearly loves a story, the reader requires some sort of suspense, something which will make him want to turn the pages. The enormous popularity of detective fiction, in books and on television, is because it has to tell stories. Novels should, among all their other attractions, satisfy the basic need to find out what happened next. And this isn't just a pleasure offered by Conan Doyle and Ruth Rendell, it's there in Shakespeare and Tolstoy, Jane Austen and Henry James.

E. M. Forster, who heaved a small sigh and said, oh dear yes, he supposed a novel does have to tell a story, knew that a plot comes from the characters. Characters must create events and not be puppets acting them out. And yet, Forster said, you can create a wonderful set of characters and they may sit around having a highly enjoyable conversation and not bother themselves to start up any sort of plot at all.

This is a danger; but I've always found the only way to trap a story is to start writing it, even if you've got no clear idea of what's going to happen next. Certainly you should start equipped with a theme, some characters to set in conflict with each other, a feeling for a place and an idea of where you might hope to arrive. No list of events, no notes, no synopsis or what film producers – who usually have no idea how such things happen – call a 'treatment' will produce a story as surely as starting to write it. You may think of a sentence, a description of one small event, which will pay off fifty pages later. If you are really in luck, the fiction writer's miracle may happen. You may invent a character with such determination and vitality that he or she will do something totally unexpected and create a far better plot than you ever dreamed possible.

Every writer attacks this problem in a different way. Some do a great deal of research. Often improbable stories are made more convincing by painstakingly accurate accounts of the geography of Budapest, or the size of the rooms in the White House. I think research is only useful after you've finished writing the book, for by then you know what you needed to find out. Some people sit at word processors, fearful objects to me, which wipe out all the valuable false starts and mistakes. Others rattle elderly typewriters. I have to face a long sheet of ruled paper and a pen. A *Rumpole* story always has three plots: one is the crime, the second concerns the old barrister's harsh home life and the third the adventures and misadventures of the pompous and self-regarding members of his chambers. So my search for plots is endless and painful. But I have found that if you can think of a character, for instance the sort of man who wears a blue suit, a shirt bought at a London airport and a striped tie, who carries a pocket calculator and frequently says things like: 'That's right', and, 'Yes, indeed', and if you sit him in Rumpole's chair and let him start to talk about his troubles, he may give you a story you would never have thought of without him.

This way of waiting for a plot to present itself means flying blind through the first twenty pages of a book and rewriting a good deal of the beginning when you've found out what the ending might be. It may mean making a few notes on the plot; but this is an activity which should be saved until you're three-quarters of the way through. Sometimes things become clear even later. I remember that the actors and the director were engaged for the series of *Paradise Postponed*, and some of the sets built, before I had any clear idea of what the ending would be. During work on *Dunster*, my latest novel, I remember going out to sit in the garden and waiting for a long time to think of the last chapter, the final twist in the hard-won story.

I would have less confidence in these methods if they hadn't been used by great storytellers in the past and yielded results. Happily, Dickens didn't use a word processor so we can tell from his manuscripts how many alterations, changes of mind and second and third thoughts he had to live through. His minimal notes show that the idea that the Dorritts might come into money (and what would happen then?) only came to him when he was halfway through writing the book. Georges Feydeau, the master of French farce, produced plots as intricate and beautifully crafted as Swiss watches. He, it seems, made no plans, drew no maps, but just sat down to write the first scene and then waited to see what would happen. It's true that the first ten minutes of a Feydeau play are the most boring, but none of the other wonders would happen without them.

The plot of a novel can be more than the device which persuades the reader to carry on with the journey. Like the composition of a painting or the construction of a symphony, it can be a vital and satisfying element in a work of art. It is the writer's attempt to impose some coherence on the chaotic nature of our world. Dreaming up plots, a novelist can know the godlike pleasure of seeing into the future and reconstructing the past, although he must also recognise the necessity, admitted by Catholic theologians, of allowing his creatures free will.

Occasionally, perhaps once in a lifetime, you may have the intoxicating pleasure of having one of your fictional stories enter the world of reality. Some years ago I thought I'd send Rumpole to appear at a court martial with the British Army in Germany. I went off to see a court martial to learn the procedure. I listened to an interesting trial in which the only evidence that a private was smoking dope was that he claimed that was what his cigarette contained. He might, perhaps, have been boasting. Armed with the knowledge of how such trials worked I involved Rumpole in a murder charge, and an entirely fictional plot which started with a sergeant being found stabbed through the heart, wearing a woman's red evening gown, outside a disco in a small town in Germany. The story was duly written, filmed and shown on television. Some years later I visited a Guards regiment in Germany where I had been invited for dinner. I was asked to go and have a drink in the Sergeants' Mess, which I duly did, and there I was asked if I'd ever visited the army before. I said that I had and that I'd seen the court martial of a young soldier accused of smoking cannabis. 'Oh no you didn't,' one of my questioners corrected me, 'you came over for that murder case there was here some years back. The one when the sergeant was found stabbed outside a disco, wearing a woman's evening dress.'

So, in the fullness of time, my dreamt-up plot had entered the real world where, so far as I know, it has stayed until this day.

Notes on the Illustrators

MICHAEL FOREMAN

Michael Foreman studied painting at the Royal College. He obtained a first-class degree and his first children's book was published while he was still a student there. After a brief sojourn as art director of *Playboy*, he went freelance and became increasingly associated with illustrated books for children. He has travelled extensively and the influence of China, India and Australia has enriched and enhanced his work. Since his first book was published in 1961, he has illustrated more than seventy books as well as writing twenty himself. He has won many awards including the prestigious Francis Williams Award and the Kate Greenaway Medal which he was awarded in 1990 for *War Boy*, a biographical account of his own childhood in war-time England.

Previous titles include:

Land of the Long White Cloud
The Saga of Erik the Viking
War Boy

World of Fairy Tales
The Boy who Sailed with Columbus

MEL CALMAN

The artist, writer and cartoonist Mel Calman was born in 1931. He studied illustration at Borough Polytechnic, St Martin's School of Art and Goldsmiths College in London. After completing National Service, he began to draw cartoons and slowly built up a series of commissions from newspapers and magazines. He has been cartoonist for the *Daily Express, Sunday Telegraph, The Observer, Sunday Times,* and *The Times.* He has also designed book jackets and advertising campaigns, and is the illustrator of several books.

Mel Calman is founder and director of The Cartoon Gallery in London, which is devoted to showing original illustrations and cartoons. He has been married twice and has two daughters. His *Who's Who* entry states his recreations as 'brooding and worrying'.

Previous titles include:

But it's My Turn to Leave You ...
How About a Little Quarrel
  Before Bed?
It's Only You That's
  Incompatible

My God
What Else Do You Do?
Calman at the Movies
Calman at the Royal Opera
  House

ANTHONY BROWNE

Anthony Browne was born in Sheffield in 1946 and grew up near Halifax in Yorkshire, where he spent much of his time drawing. He graduated from Leeds College of Art and later lectured there in graphic design. He then worked in Manchester as a medical artist, drawing specimens and post-mortems. He also designed cards for Gordon Fraser Greeting Cards for several years. His first picture-book was published in 1976. Since then he has published numerous books and received a number of awards including the Emil/Kurt Maschler Award (twice), the Kate Greenaway Medal, the New York Times Best Illustrated Book and the Boston Globe Award Honour Book. He has been invited to the USA, Canada, France and Australia and he is one of the few British artists to have made a real breakthrough in international markets. He lives in Kent with his wife and two young children.

Previous titles include:

Look What I've Got
Hansel and Gretel
Gorilla
Willy the Wimp
Piggybook
Kirsty Knows Best

Alice's Adventures in
*   Wonderland*
The Tunnel
The Trail of Stones
Changes

MAIRI HEDDERWICK

Mairi Hedderwick was born in Renfrewshire in 1939. At the age of seventeen, she took a job as a mother's help on the Hebridean island of Coll. She returned to the mainland to attend Edinburgh College of Art and then taught for a while. She married and had two children and, in 1969, she and her husband decided to move to Coll. Her *Katie Morag* series of books are loosely based on her life there.

The family returned to the mainland in 1973 and she began illustrating books for other authors. She also worked as a social development worker, taught and did freelance art work. *Katie Morag Delivers the Mail* was published in 1984 and was taken up as an excellent example of non-sexist children's fiction, mainly because of the tractor-fixing, dungaree-wearing Granny character.

Previous titles include:

*Katie Morag Delivers the
    Mail*
*Katie Morag and the
    New Pier*
*Katie Morag and the
    Tiresome Ted*
A Kist o' Whistles

*Peedie Pebbles' Summer or
    Winter Book*
An Eye on the Hebrides
*The Old Woman Who Lived in
    a Vine*
Hands Off Our School!

ANN ROSS PATERSON

Ann Ross Paterson studied at Edinburgh Art College. She has designed all the print for the Book Festival since 1983 and this year she has also illustrated the poster, the diary and the cover of this book.

Her graphics and illustrations appear on many books, biscuit tins, jam jars and whisky bottles, and promote numerous arts events and festivals around Scotland.

ALBERT UDERZO

Albert Uderzo started illustrating when he was fourteen. In 1959, after having worked for various magazines, he collaborated with his writer friend, René Goscinny, to create *The Adventures of Asterix the Gaul*. Asterix was first published in the French weekly magazine *Pilote* and its phenomenal success put an end to the American monopoly of comic strips.

Since Goscinny's death in 1977, Albert has been responsible for both illustrations and text. He is so familiar with the characters that he easily maintains the spirit of the previous stories. It takes about nine months to write and illustrate every adventure. Up to 12,000 illustrations have already been drawn for the thirty-one titles in the Asterix collection. Over 140 million books have been sold worldwide and they have been translated into thirty languages.

Previous titles include:

Asterix at the Olympic Games
Asterix and the Golden Sickle
Asterix and the Goths
Asterix and the Magic Carpet

Asterix the Gladiator
Fantastic Asterix
The Roman Conspiracy

TONY ROSS

Tony Ross was born in 1938 in London. He trained at Liverpool School of Art and has worked as a cartoonist, a graphic designer and the art director of an advertising agency. He was Senior Lecturer in Art at Manchester Polytechnic.

Over the past few years, Tony Ross has become one of the best known creators of original and traditional picture books and his work has been sold all over the world. In 1976 *Goldilocks and the Three Bears* was voted one of the best books of the year by the Federation of Children's Book Groups. Since then he has produced a series of highly popular fairy-tales, re-told and updated in his own inimitable style, which combines a humorous text with a flamboyant use of line and colour. As well as picture books, Tony Ross has also illustrated juvenile fiction titles for several publishers in the UK, France and the USA. Many of his books have been published in up to ten different foreign language editions.

Previous titles include:

Oscar Got the Blame
Super Dooper Jezebel
The Three Pigs
Well I Never
Anyone Seen Harry Lately?
I Want to Be
*Dr Xargle's Book of
    Earth Relations*

Dr Xargle's Book of Earthlets
Hansel and Gretel
The Cherry Tree
Bubble Trouble
Big, Bad Barney Bear
*Alice's Adventures in
    Wonderland*
Duck Soup Farm